Microsoft Dynamics CRM 2011 Reporting

Everything you need to know to work with reports in Dynamics CRM 2011

Damian Sinay

BIRMINGHAM - MUMBAI

Microsoft Dynamics CRM 2011 Reporting

First published: June 2013

Production Reference: 1180613

Published by Packt Publishing Ltd.
Livery Place
35 Livery Street
Birmingham B3 2PB, UK.

ISBN 978-1-84968-230-5

www.packtpub.com

Cover Image by Sandeep Babu (sandyjb@gmail.com)

Credits

Author
Damian Sinay

Reviewers
Nishant Rana
James Wood

Acquisition Editor
Vinay Argekar

Commissioning Editor
Shreerang Deshpande

Lead Technical Editor
Mayur Hule

Technical Editors
Sharvari Baet
Jeeten Handu
Veena Pagare
Akshata Patil
Kaustubh S. Mayekar

Copy Editors
Insiya Morbiwala
Aditya Nair
Alfida Paiva
Laxmi Subramanian

Project Coordinator
Leena Purkait

Proofreaders
Aaron Nash
Paul Hindle

Indexer
Tejal R. Soni

Graphics
Abhinash Sahu

Production Coordinator
Conidon Miranda

Cover Work
Conidon Miranda

About the Author

Damian Sinay has over 15 years experience in the software development and IT industry. He started working with the .NET framework when its first Version 1.0 was in the beta stage. In 2002, he won first prize in the "Building solutions based on XML Web Services" contest, which spanned across Latin America, by Microsoft. In 2006, he wrote his first book in his native language (Spanish) on web services with C# development.

He started working with CRM solutions prior to the first release of Microsoft Dynamics CRM's initial version. Since then, he has exclusively been developing and implementing solutions for Dynamics CRM and SharePoint. He is certified in Versions 3.0, 4.0, and 2011 including development, installation, configuration, and implementation of Dynamics CRM. He has around 18 Microsoft certifications (MCP) in SQL, C#, ASP.NET, TFS, Project, CRM, and SharePoint 2007 and 2010. Among many other things, he has co-authored the Dynamics CRM unleashed books for Versions 4.0 and 2011.

He held the Microsoft Most Valuable Professional (MVP) award in Dynamics CRM in 2012 and serves as the CEO of Remoting Coders, a Microsoft Partner company that is turning 10 years old in 2013, providing solutions using Microsoft products and technologies.

You can contact Damian at damian@sinay.com.ar, follow him on Twitter at @damiansinay, and can also read the blog at http://www.remotingcoders.com/Blogsite/.

I would like to especially thank my wife Carina Godoy de Sinay and my kids who have been positive and unconditional supporters.

I would also like to thank my clients, my colleagues, Microsoft MVPs, the Microsoft CRM product team, and my partners who have provided invaluable opportunities for me to expand my knowledge and shape my career.

About the Reviewers

Nishant Rana currently works at Microsoft Services Global Delivery (MSGD). He has done his specialization in the Microsoft .NET technology and has been actively involved with it since its release. His main focus area has been Microsoft Dynamics CRM and SharePoint. He is a Microsoft Certified Technology Specialist and an IT professional in Dynamics and SharePoint, and a MCAD (Application Developer) for .NET.

He has also reviewed the book entitled *Microsoft Dynamics CRM 2011 Application Design, Mahendar Pal, Packt Publishing*.

You can contact Nishant via his website or Twitter account:

```
http://nishantrana.wordpress.com/
```

```
https://twitter.com/nishantranaCRM
```

> I would like to thank my family and my friends for their love, care, and support.

James Wood is a consultant at Gap Consulting with skills in the end-to-end implementation of enterprise-level Microsoft Dynamics CRM solutions. He graduated from the University of Huddersfield with a First Class degree in Computer Games Programming before making the switch to business applications.

He has worked with Microsoft Dynamics CRM for three years and is an able developer of bespoke applications. He has worked on a number of small to large implementations in sectors including local and regional government, education, defense, banking, manufacturing, and welfare.

He has also worked as a technical reviewer for *Microsoft Dynamics CRM 2011 Application Design* and *Microsoft Dynamics CRM 2011: An expert cookbook for securing, customizing, and extending your CRM apps.*

You can read his blog at www.woodsworkblog.wordpress.com.

I would like to thank my family and friends for everything — especially Mum, Dad, Rob, and Chloë.

www.PacktPub.com

Support files, eBooks, discount offers and more

You might want to visit www.PacktPub.com for support files and downloads related to your book.

Did you know that Packt offers eBook versions of every book published, with PDF and ePub files available? You can upgrade to the eBook version at www.PacktPub.com and as a print book customer, you are entitled to a discount on the eBook copy. Get in touch with us at service@packtpub.com for more details.

At www.PacktPub.com, you can also read a collection of free technical articles, sign up for a range of free newsletters and receive exclusive discounts and offers on Packt books and eBooks.

http://PacktLib.PacktPub.com

Do you need instant solutions to your IT questions? PacktLib is Packt's online digital book library. Here, you can access, read and search across Packt's entire library of books.

Why Subscribe?

- Fully searchable across every book published by Packt
- Copy and paste, print and bookmark content
- On demand and accessible via web browser

Free Access for Packt account holders

If you have an account with Packt at www.PacktPub.com, you can use this to access PacktLib today and view nine entirely free books. Simply use your login credentials for immediate access.

Instant Updates on New Packt Books

Get notified! Find out when new books are published by following @PacktEnterprise on Twitter, or the *Packt Enterprise* Facebook page.

Table of Contents

Preface

Microsoft Dynamics CRM 2011 Reporting is a practical reference guide that provides you with a number of different options you can use to create and empower the reporting capabilities of Dynamics CRM. This will give you a good grounding for using the reports in your Dynamics CRM 2011 implementations.

What this book covers

Chapter 1, Introduction to Reporting in Microsoft Dynamics CRM explains the different types of reports we can use in Dynamics CRM. Further, it explains SQL Server Reporting Services (SSRS) and how to install the Dynamics CRM 2011 Extensions. It also covers how to install the Microsoft Dynamics CRM 2011 Report Authoring Extension, which we are going to use and explain later in this book.

Chapter 2, Database Basics explains the entity-relationship model of Dynamics CRM; we will review the basic and advanced commands of the SQL language as well as the FETCH XML language that we will need to use in order to create the queries we will use in our reports. We are going to keep using these two languages in the following chapters.

Chapter 3, Creating Your First Report in CRM helps us to create our first report using the Report Wizard and also to export the report to be edited with Visual Studio 2008, where we will make some customizations to reupload the report in Dynamics CRM. We will also see how to publish the report to be visible on the Reporting Server manager for external use.

Chapter 4, SQL Server Report Builder helps us to create our first report using the Report Builder and shows us the features we can use that were not available in the standard CRM Report Wizard. We will also create an advanced report using the Map Wizard, where we will show the records held by the USA.

Chapter 5, Creating Contextual Reports explains the advanced tools and controls we can use to create reports with Visual Studio. We will review the CRM Report parameters and the chart controls. This chapter explains the differences between the data source and datasets, and finally looks at how to use the groups, drill-down and collapsible controls in reports.

Chapter 6, Creating Inline Reports shows us how we can embed a report inside any entity form by creating a custom solution that uses an HTML web resource. We will also see how to implement this custom solution on the account entity using the account overview report. We will then review the development toolkit, which will help us work in a more organized manner with custom CRM solutions to get the benefit of IntelliSense. The deployment capability also allows us to integrate our source code with a source controller software, such as the Team Foundation server.

Chapter 7, Using Reports and Charts in Dashboard shows us how we can integrate a report in a CRM Dashboard and explains the chart basics as well as more advanced details; this is always a good option to display important information about the CRM system if we don't want to use reports.

Chapter 8, Advance Custom Reporting and Automation shows us how we can integrate a custom ASP.NET or Silverlight application to show a dynamic or more sophisticated report inside Dynamics CRM 2011. We will look at the different ways to bind CRM data by using early or late binding methods, and finally we will look at some ways to automate SSRS reports by either using scheduling or by automating export report generation with code.

Chapter 9, Failure Recovery and Best Practices shows us how we can troubleshoot different authentication issues we might face when working with reports in Dynamics CRM, as well as the different ways to improve the report development performance and deployment by using some of the best practices for SQL Reporting Services.

Chapter 10, Mobile Client shows us the new features of Dynamics CRM and SQL Server 2012 to show and run reports on mobile devices, such as iPhone, iPad, and Surface. We will look at how to configure the IFD authentication so we can give external users access to our on-premise CRM environment.

Appendix, Expression Snippets shows us some basic expressions and how we can use them in our reports; we will learn how to use constants, variables, and functions, as well as using external .NET assemblies by using the references. Finally, we will look at the user interaction controls that will help us interact with the users.

What you need for this book

- Windows Server Standard Edition 2008 R2 or 2012
- SQL Server 2012 with SP1/2008 R2 with SP2
- Visual Studio 2008/2010 installed by the SQL Server development tools
- Dynamics CRM 2011 with RU 13 and/or CRM Online
- Visual Studio 2012 for custom reports in ASP.NET and Silverlight

Who this book is for

This book is an indispensable guide for users and developers new to Dynamics CRM Reports and SQL Server Reporting Services, and who are looking to get a good grounding in using the reporting capabilities of Dynamics CRM 2011. It's assumed that you will already have some experience in HTML and JavaScript to build advanced reports, but no previous programming experience is required to build and learn how to create some basic to intermediate reports, which will be used for the exercises within this book.

Conventions

In this book, you will find a number of styles of text that distinguish between different kinds of information. Here are some examples of these styles, and an explanation of their meaning.

Code words in text are shown as follows: "To group you add the `aggregate='true'` attribute to the `fetch` node."

A block of code is set as follows:

```
<fetch version="1.0" mapping="logical" distinct="false">
  <entity name="account">
    <attribute name="telephone1" />
  </entity>
</fetch>
```

When we wish to draw your attention to a particular part of a code block, the relevant lines or items are set in bold:

```
DataTable accounts = new DataTable("Accounts");
        accounts.Columns.Add("name");
        accounts.Columns.Add("accountid");
        string fetchQuery = @"
            <fetch distinct='false' mapping='logical' >
```

Any command-line input or output is written as follows:

```
declare @name as varchar(160)
declare @revenue as money
```

New terms and **important words** are shown in bold. Words that you see on the screen, in menus or dialog boxes for example, appear in the text like this: "Check the checkbox that says **I accept this license agreement** and click on **I Accept** to continue".

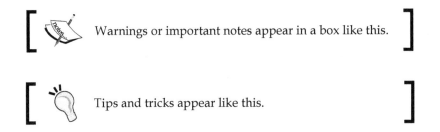

Warnings or important notes appear in a box like this.

Tips and tricks appear like this.

Reader feedback

Feedback from our readers is always welcome. Let us know what you think about this book—what you liked or may have disliked. Reader feedback is important for us to develop titles that you really get the most out of.

To send us general feedback, simply send an e-mail to feedback@packtpub.com, and mention the book title via the subject of your message.

If there is a topic that you have expertise in and you are interested in either writing or contributing to a book, see our author guide on www.packtpub.com/authors.

Customer support

Now that you are the proud owner of a Packt book, we have a number of things to help you to get the most from your purchase.

Downloading the example code

You can download the example code files for all Packt books you have purchased from your account at http://www.packtpub.com. If you purchased this book elsewhere, you can visit http://www.packtpub.com/support and register to have the files e-mailed directly to you.

Errata

Although we have taken every care to ensure the accuracy of our content, mistakes do happen. If you find a mistake in one of our books—maybe a mistake in the text or the code—we would be grateful if you would report this to us. By doing so, you can save other readers from frustration and help us improve subsequent versions of this book. If you find any errata, please report them by visiting http://www.packtpub.com/submit-errata, selecting your book, clicking on the **errata submission form** link, and entering the details of your errata. Once your errata are verified, your submission will be accepted and the errata will be uploaded on our website, or added to any list of existing errata, under the Errata section of that title. Any existing errata can be viewed by selecting your title from http://www.packtpub.com/support.

Piracy

Piracy of copyright material on the Internet is an ongoing problem across all media. At Packt, we take the protection of our copyright and licenses very seriously. If you come across any illegal copies of our works, in any form, on the Internet, please provide us with the location address or website name immediately so that we can pursue a remedy.

Please contact us at copyright@packtpub.com with a link to the suspected pirated material.

We appreciate your help in protecting our authors, and our ability to bring you valuable content.

Questions

You can contact us at questions@packtpub.com if you are having a problem with any aspect of the book, and we will do our best to address it.

1
Introduction to Reporting in Microsoft Dynamics CRM

Microsoft Dynamics CRM 2011 makes extensive use of reporting, which we will be covering through this entire book. Reporting is a very important piece of any system that is heavily used by managers or upper management roles, such as the CEO and COO, of any enterprise. In this chapter we will cover:

- CRM report types
- CRM report settings
- SQL Reporting Services versions
- Installation and configuration of Reporting Services Extension
- Installation and configuration of Report Authoring Extension (used for Visual Studio development)

CRM report types

Microsoft Dynamics CRM 2011 allows different types of reports; not only can the SQL Reporting Services reports be used, but other custom reports, such as Crystal Reports, ASP.NET, or Silverlight reports can also be integrated.

Dynamics CRM can manage the following types of reports:

- RDL files, which are SQL Reporting Services reports
- External links to external applications such as Crystal Reports, ASP.NET, or Silverlight reports
- Native CRM dashboards with charts

The RDL files can be created in either of the following two ways:

- By using the Report Wizard
- By using Visual Studio

Dynamics CRM 2011 comes with 54 predefined reports out of the box; 25 of them are main reports and 29 are subreports. If for some reason you don't see any report as shown in the following screenshot, it means Dynamics CRM 2011 Reporting Extensions were not installed. This is something that can only happen for on-premise environments; if you are working with CRM Online, you don't need to be worried about any report-extension-deployment tasks.

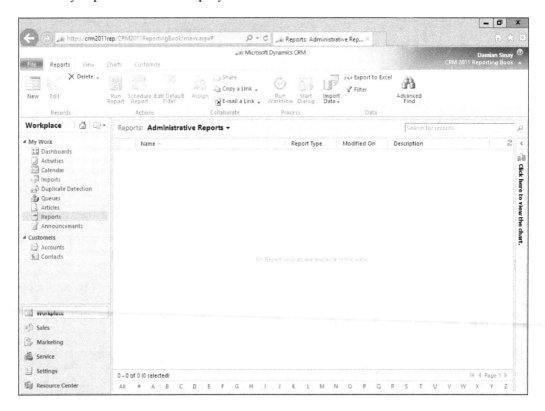

CRM report settings

Reports in Dynamics CRM have the following settings or categories that you can access by clicking on the **Edit** button of each report, as shown in the following screenshot:

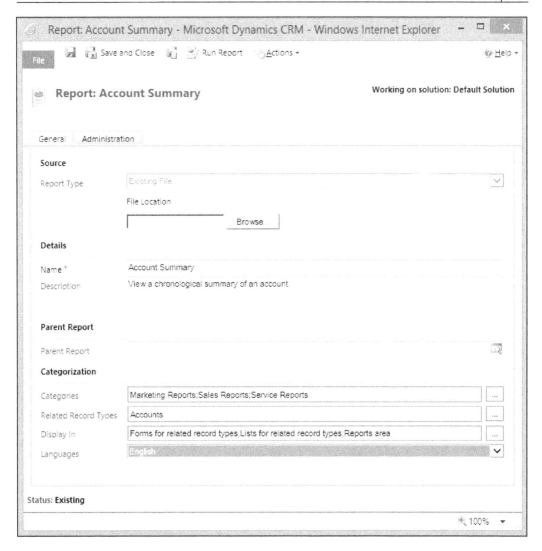

In the **Report: Account Summary** window you will see two tabs, **General** and **Administration**.

The **Administration** tab will show the name of the owner of the report, when the report was created or updated and who did it, and whether it is viewable to the user or the entire organization.

In the **General** tab, you will see the name of the report and the description. If it is a subreport, we will see the parent report displayed. Lastly, in the **Categorization** section, you can see the following settings:

- **Categories**
- **Related Record Types**
- **Display in**
- **Languages**

We will study each of these settings in detail.

Categories

By default, there are four categories created out of the box in every CRM organization:

- **Administrative Reports**
- **Marketing Reports**
- **Sales Reports**
- **Service Reports**

You can change, add, or remove these categories by navigating to **Settings** | **Administration** | **System Settings** | **Reporting** as shown in the following screenshot:

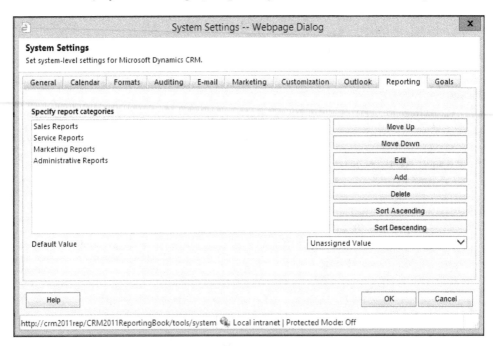

These report categories are used so that you can filter reports by each category when the predefined views are available in the main **Reports** interface, as shown in the following screenshot:

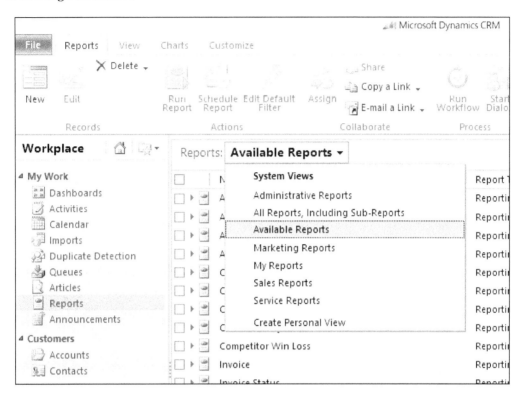

Notice that if you add a new category, you will also have to create the view as it won't be created automatically.

Related Record Types

The **Related Record Types** option allows you to select what entities you want the report to be displayed under.

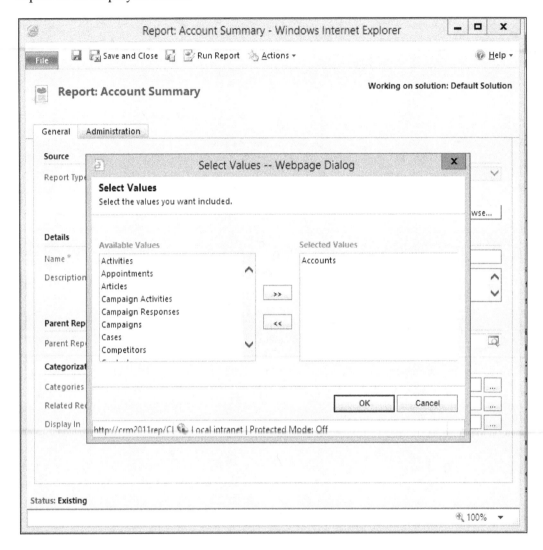

The reports will be listed under the **Run Report** button that is on the Ribbon. There are two locations where the report will be listed on the entities you selected: the home page grid and the form.

The home page grid is where you see all the records of an entity (depending on the view you selected) as shown in the following screenshot:

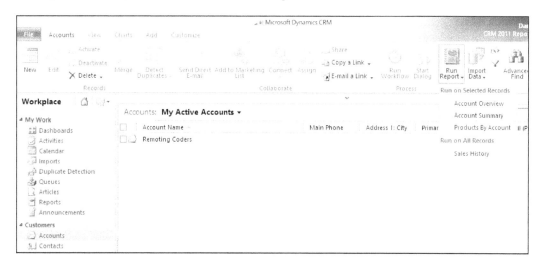

Almost every entity in Dynamics CRM has a **Run Report** button. As you can see, there are some reports that can run on the selected records and there are others that only run on all records. We will see how to configure this in detail when we go deeper into report development with Visual Studio in *Chapter 5, Creating Contextual Reports*.

The form is the second place where the **Run Report** button is located and it is visible on the form record that you will see when you open a record; the report will only affect that record.

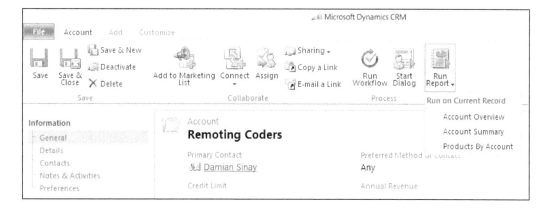

Display in

As we saw in the **Related Record Types** option, we can decide here where we want to show our report. The options are:

- Forms for related record types
- Lists for related record types
- The **Reports** area

The first option will make the report available on the **Run Report** button, which is on the form ribbon of an entity record as we have seen earlier.

The lists for the **Related Record Types** option appears on the home page grid ribbon button.

The **Reports** area refers to the main reporting interface that is in the **Workplace**.

Languages

This last option of the **Categorization** section allows us to specify the language of the report. We have the option of selecting all the languages on the list if you want your single report to be displayed in any of these languages. This is helpful if we have the different language packs installed on the CRM Server and the organization has people from different countries who understand different languages. By default all the reports are based on the local language.

 This option might not be visible on your installation if you don't have any other language installed on the system.

SQL reporting services versions

The first version of reporting services was released as a separate download for SQL 2000. It was in the SQL 2005 version that it was integrated in the SQL Server installation media and became an optional feature of the SQL Server setup.

I remember that when I first installed SQL Reporting Services 2000, the setup was very complicated and required touching some XML files manually. It was in the 2005 version that it included a very nice application called **Reporting Services Configuration Manager** to help set up and deploy, which has been improving with every version to make this task much easier.

The 2000 and 2005 versions required **Internet Information Services (IIS)** to be installed on the server to be used by the report manager and report web services. However, the 2008 and 2012 versions come with their own HTTP server and don't make use of the IIS.

There is an important difference between the versions of SQL Server and Visual Studio. Basically, the last version of SQL 2012 is one version behind Visual Studio as currently there is no support for the Report Server Project Templates in Visual Studio 2012. The following table shows this discrepancy:

SQL Server	Visual Studio	CRM Server
2005	Visual Studio 2005	4.0
2008	Visual Studio 2005	4.0 and 2011
2008 R2	Visual Studio 2008	4.0 and 2011
2012	Visual Studio 2010	4.0 and 2011

Dynamics CRM 2011 was originally designed to work with Windows Server 2008 R2 and SQL Server 2008 R2. Installing Dynamics CRM 2011 on Windows Server 2012 with SQL Server 2012 is very challenging; Daniel Cai, a fellow Microsoft MVP in Dynamics CRM, has written the necessary steps and workarounds in his article at `http://danielcai.blogspot.com.ar/2012/05/install-crm-2011-on-windows-server-8.html`.

As we can see in the `http://support.microsoft.com/default.aspx?kbid=2791312` link, there is upcoming support for Windows 2012 with the Update Rollup 13, which will be available on the Windows Update.

In this book, I have decided to use the latest Microsoft versions, Windows Server 2012 and SQL Server 2012, to take the benefits of the latest features and improvements. I will mention in this book whenever a specific feature is different from the previous versions, as some implementations might still use the 2008 R2 versions.

At the time of writing this book, CRM Online is using SQL Server 2012.

Some of the benefits of using SQL Server 2012 with Dynamics CRM 2011 are as follows:

- Support for the mobile client with the SQL Server 2012 Service Pack 1
- Alerts directly from the reporting-service control
- Better performance

There is also another version of SQL Reporting Services that uses the same concept but is hosted in the cloud of Windows Azure; however, this version can't be used with Dynamics CRM directly.

Regardless of the edition, SQL Reporting Services has four main components:

- SQL Server databases
- Windows Service
- Report Manager website
- Report Server Web service

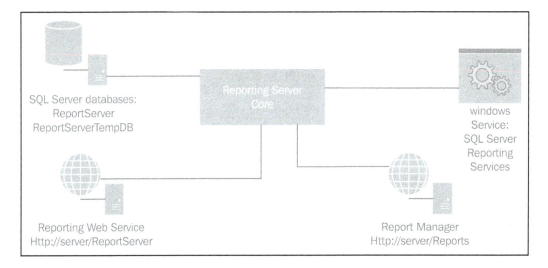

SQL Server databases:
ReportServer
ReportServerTempDB

Reporting Server Core

windows
Service:
SQL Server
Reporting
Services

Reporting Web Service
Http://server/ReportServer

Report Manager
Http://server/Reports

SQL Server databases

There are two databases that are used by the SQL Reporting Services – ReportServer and ReportServerTempDB. All the reports and configurations are stored in the first database, and the second one is used to store temporary data and improve the service performance by caching the user sessions. Notice that these databases' names are set by default and a **Database administrator** (**DBA**) might change the names using the Reporting Services Configuration Manager.

Windows Service

The Windows Service is used to automatically generate scheduled reports that can be scheduled with the Report Manager website or the CRM interface, as we will see in *Chapter 8*, *Advance Custom Reporting and Automation*. You can see this Windows Service in the Windows Services tool with the name of **SQL Server Reporting Services (MSSQLSERVER)**, where **MSSQLSERVER** will be the name of the SQL Server instance you are running.

Report Manager website

The Report Manager is the web-user interface in which a user can see, create, and run reports by usually going to a URL such as `http://<servername>/Reports`. From this interface, the administrator can also give and assign permissions to the reports as well as configure and run the reports directly.

Report Server Web service

The Report Server Web service is the web service end point where a developer can integrate with other custom applications. Usually, by going to a URL such as `http://servername/ReportServer`, a developer can create another user interface to do everything the Report Manager website can do, but with a custom interface or application such as a Windows or WPF app. This is the URL that Visual Studio and the Report Builder use to connect and interact with the reporting services to run and deploy reports. This web service is very useful if you want to automate some of the export report features, such as to automate the generation of a PDF document by executing a report. An example of one of the end points exposed can be found at `http://<servername>/ReportServer/ReportService2010.asmx`; there are other ASMX files for compatibility with previous versions, such as `ReportService2006.asmx` and `ReportService2005.asmx`.

Installation and configuration of Reporting Services Extensions

If the Dynamics CRM 2011 Reporting Extensions were not installed during the initial setup of Dynamics CRM, you can install them manually later by executing the `SetupSrsDataConnector.exe` file that is located in the `Server\amd64\SrsDataConnector` folder of the Dynamics CRM 2011 installation media. It is important to know that this needs to be installed on the server where the SQL Reporting Services is installed.

To install the Reporting Services extensions, follow the given steps:

1. Execute the file `SetupSrsDataConnector.exe`.

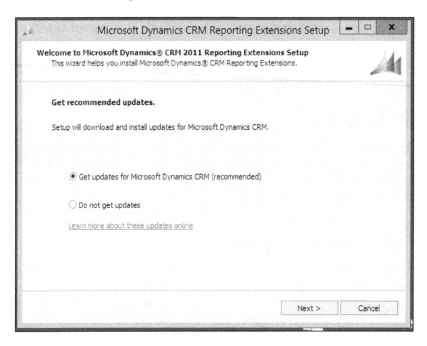

2. Click on **Next** to continue.

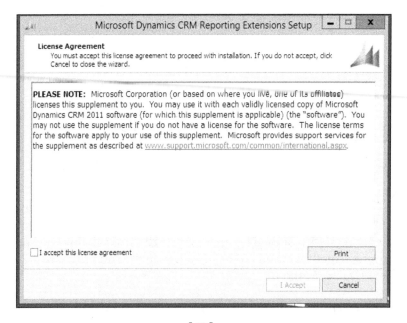

3. Check the checkbox **I accept the license agreement** and click on **I Accept** to continue.

4. Click on **Install** when the **Download** and **Install** required components window pop ups and then click on **Next** to continue.

5. By default the setup will show the SQL Server used by CRM 2011; choose the suggested server name and click on **Next** to continue.

6. Choose the suggested instance and click on **Next** to continue.

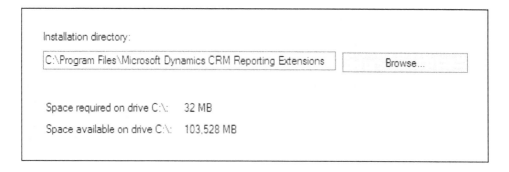

7. Select the installation directory or leave the default suggested location and click on **Next** to continue.

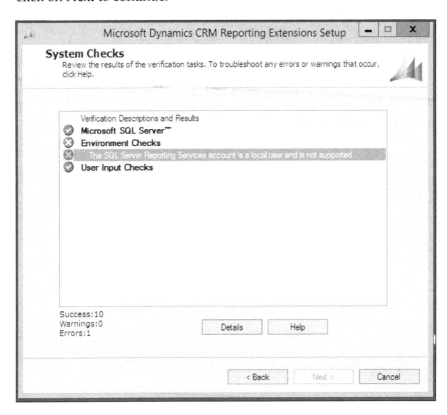

The setup will validate the system, and in case of any errors, it will be displayed.

In this case, the error shown refers to a typical SQL 2012 SRS installation, where the local account ReportServer is used by default. We will need to change the reporting service account by using the Reporting Services Configuration Manager tool and either use a domain account specifically created for this purpose or use the **Network Service** local account.

 We can use the Network Service account because this account is also the computer account on the domain controller (Active Directory). This means that at the end it is also a domain account.

8. If we use the Network Service account, we will see a warning as shown in the following screenshot:

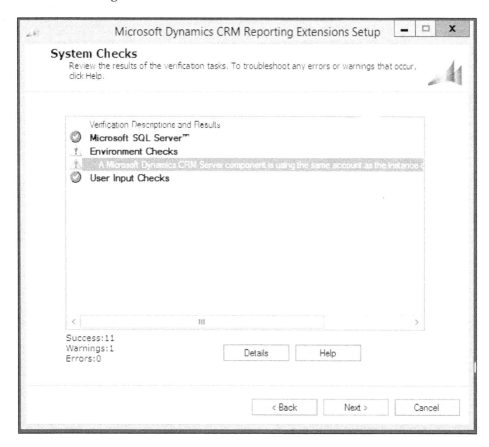

9. Click on **Next** to continue.

10. As we can see in the warning page, the SQL Server Reporting Service will need to be restarted; therefore we need to be sure that nobody would need it while installing this component. Click on **Next** to continue.

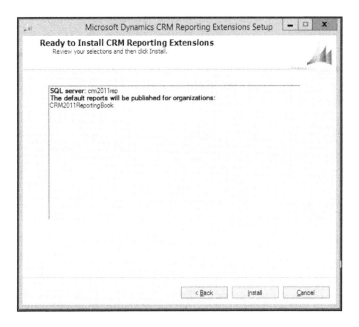

11. Now we are ready to install the extensions, so click on **Install** to continue. The setup will take a few minutes to complete.

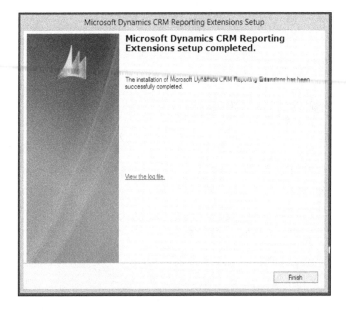

12. Click on **Finish** to close the installer. To validate that we have deployed the reports successfully, we can go to the CRM Web interface and click on **Reports**. We should now see all the reports installed as shown in the following screenshot:

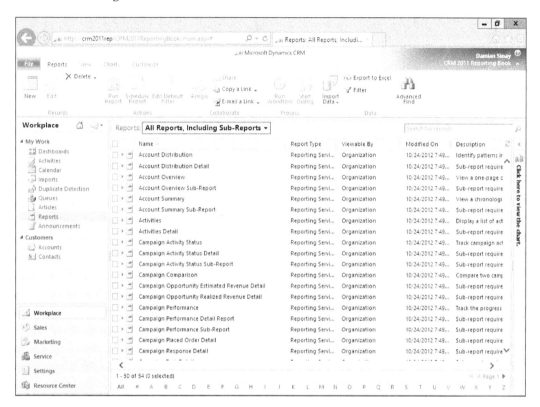

It is very important that we also validate this page from another computer that is neither the CRM Server nor the SQL Server, to be sure that the reports work properly for the users. Issues in the configurations would make the reports work well only on the server but not on the user machines. In *Chapter 9, Failure Recovery and Best Practices,* we review some of the common issues and solutions related to the reporting services' authentication issues.

After installing the Reporting Services Extensions, it is also recommended to install the latest rollup updates (service packs) to match the same rollup update as the CRM Server. At the time of writing, the latest rollup update for Dynamics CRM 2011 was number 13 and it can be downloaded using either the **Windows Update** option or by going to `http://www.microsoft.com/en-us/download/details.aspx?id=37133` and downloading the `CRM2011-Srs-KB2791312-ENU-amd64.exe` file.

To check what rollup update version you have installed and/
or see all the different rollup updates that are available, you can
refer to this blog article:

```
http://blogs.msdn.com/b/crminthefield/
archive/2012/01/12/microsoft-dynamics-crm-4-
0-and-2011-update-rollup-release-dates-build-
numbers-and-collateral.aspx
```

Installation and configuration of Report Authoring Extension (Visual Studio development)

The Report Authoring Extension component is essential if you are planning to develop SQL Reporting Service reports with Visual Studio 2008; it will add the necessary FetchXML data connector. As we will see in detail in *Chapter 3, Creating Your First Report in CRM*, the reports that are generated with the Report Wizard use this connector. So if you want to update any of the reports generated by the Report Wizard, you will need to have these extensions installed on your development machine.

The extensions require SQL Server 2008 developer tools to be installed; after the Update Rollup 13, you can now install it on the SQL Server 2010 developer tools. Before Update Rollup 13, the extensions were not compatible with the tools installed by SQL Server 2012; this is because SQL 2012 uses Visual Studio 2010 instead of Visual Studio 2008, which is the version that is required by default. After the Update Rollup 13, support for the Visual Studio 2010 that comes with SQL 2012 has been added.

At the time of writing, there is no known version of the developer tools that is compatible with Visual Studio 2012.

To install this extension, you will need to download the Microsoft Dynamics CRM 2011 Report Authoring Extension from the Microsoft downloads website or by going to the following URL:

```
http://www.microsoft.com/en-us/download/details.aspx?id=27823
```

The following are the steps to install and configure Report Authoring Extension:

1. Download the file with the name CRM2011-Bids-ENU-i386.exe.

   After downloading and executing this file, you will be prompted to select a folder where the files will be extracted to and the following first dialog will appear:

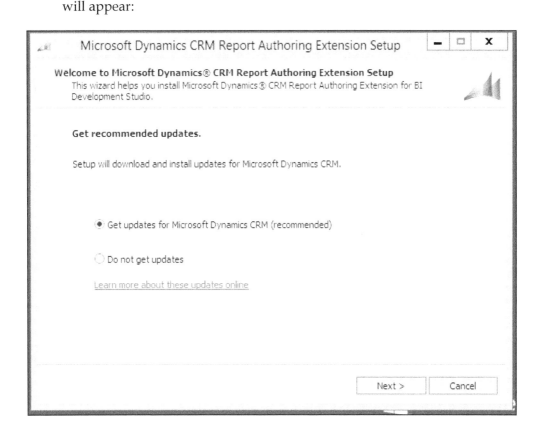

2. Select the option **Get updates for Microsoft Dynamics CRM (recommended)** and click on **Next** to continue.

3. Click on **Next** to continue.

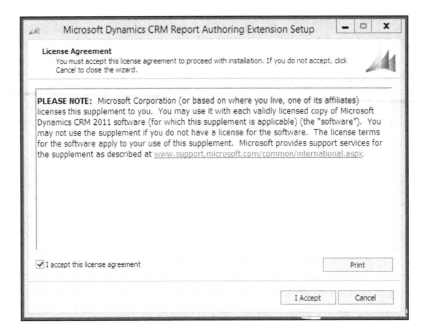

4. Check the checkbox that says **I accept this license agreement** and click on **I Accept** to continue.

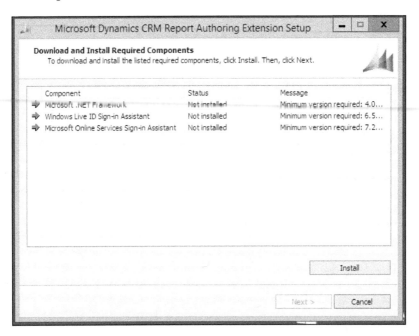

If you try to install this tool on a Windows 2012 server, where you have the SQL Server Data tools installed, you will need to install the Windows Identity Foundation 3.5 server role first or this installer will fail.

5. Install the required components by clicking on the **Install** button. After that, click on **Next** to continue.

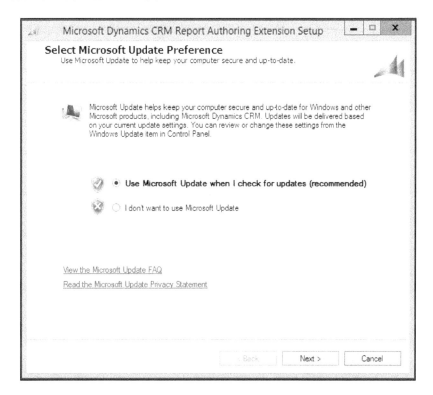

6. Select the recommended option and click on **Next** to continue.

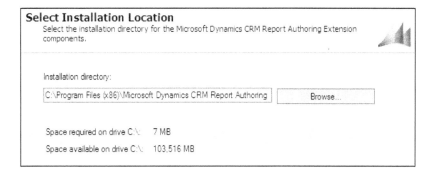

7. Leave the default location as it appears or select the location where you want the component to be installed, and click on **Next**.

8. The setup will check whether everything is okay in the system before letting you start the installation; click on **Next** to continue.

9. Now click on **Install**.

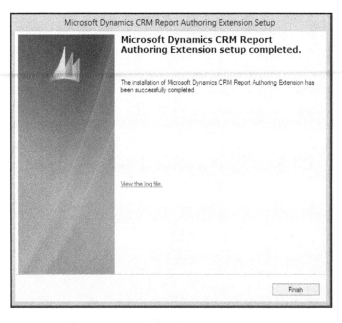

If there is any error, you will be able to see the details by clicking on the **View the log file** link.

10. Click on **Finish** to close the setup application.

You can validate whether the Report Authoring Extensions are well installed by looking at the data source types in Visual Studio 2008, where **Microsoft Dynamics CRM Fetch** should be listed as an option.

Summary

In this chapter we have explained the different types of reports we can use in Dynamics CRM. Further, we have learned about SQL Server Reporting Services (SSRS) and how to install the Dynamics CRM 2011 connector. We have also covered how to install the Microsoft Dynamics CRM 2011 Report Authoring Extension, which we are going to use and explain later in this book.

The next chapter will show the entity relationship model of dynamics CRM and review the basic and advanced commands of the SQL language as well as the FetchXML language.

2
Database Basics

Microsoft Dynamics CRM 2011 makes extensive use of the database that we are going to look at through the entire book.

In this chapter we will cover:

- **ERD (Entity Relationships Diagrams)** basics
- SQL basics
- SQL advanced
- FetchXML

ERD basics

Microsoft Dynamics CRM 2011 uses SQL Server as its database backend. There are two main databases that are created after the CRM server is initially set up. The `MSCRM_CONFIG` database, which is the one that holds different organizations' data and general configurations. The other is a database for the organization itself, with a name like `<organizationname>_MSCRM`. Depending on the number of CRM organizations you have in the system, you will have the same number of databases ending with `_MSCRM` with similar database schemas. The only difference between the organizations' databases would be the specific customizations on the entities and fields.

Microsoft Dynamics CRM 2011 uses the concept of entities to name, which in a database language would be like a table. An entity is usually a noun such as a person or house. Dynamics CRM comes with lot of entities already created in the system, such as `Account`, `Contact`, and `Invoice`.

As in any table, the entities contain fields. Each field represents an attribute in the entity. Some examples of fields are `First Name`, `Name`, and `Address`.

Dynamics CRM 2011 has the following types of fields:

- Single line of text
- Option set
- Two options
- Whole number
- Floating point number
- Decimal number
- Currency
- Multiple lines of texts
- Date and time
- Lookup

 You can go to `http://technet.microsoft.com/en-us/library/gg328507.aspx` for a reference of the types of fields used in the Microsoft Dynamics CRM SDK.

Dynamics CRM is a structured system and hence it manages everything in entities. Once you create a field in CRM, you won't be able to change the type of field as you would be able to in Microsoft SharePoint.

For any entity you create in CRM, the system will create different objects in SQL: it will create two tables, one with the name of the entity plus the `Base` suffix and another table with the same name plus the `ExtensionBase` suffix.

For example, if we create an entity called `Project`, the following two tables will be created:

- `New_ProjectBase`
- `New_ProjectExtensionBase`

Notice that the `New_` prefix comes with the default publisher of the solution on which we created the custom entity, and can be changed by creating another publisher.

Apart from the tables, there will be two views that CRM will also create in the SQL Server database:

- `New_project`
- `Filterednew_project`

The first view, `new_project`, will return the join of the two tables `New_ProjectBase` and `New_ProjectExtensionBase` as these two tables have a one-to-one relationship because they share the same primary key, `new_projectId`. All the IDs in CRM are GUIDS, which are unique identifiers.

The second view is similar to the first one but with the addition of capacity to control the security of the results based on the calling user. So if this view is selected by a customer service representative, it will return only the records this user has permissions to see, and the first view won't validate any permissions and would always return all the records.

For these reasons, it is recommended to always use the filtered views when querying the records in our reports. That way we can be sure that we will only display information that the user who runs the report is allowed to see.

Another benefit of using views is that you not only get the fields of one table, such as the `Base` table, but also the fields from the `ExtensionBase` suffix plus the option set values that are also stored on a separated table.

Relationship types

The entities in Dynamics CRM can be related in the following ways:

- 1:N (one-to-many)
- N:1 (many-to-one)
- N:N (many-to-many)

> For normalization purposes, Dynamics CRM doesn't allow 1:1 (one-to-one) relationships.
>
> If you want to review the ERD of your CRM system and custom entities, you can download the solution I have published in CodePlex, which is located at `http://crm2011erd.codeplex.com/`.

When you go to the Dynamics CRM interface having the system administrator or system customizer role, you can go to **Settings | Customizations | Customize the System**. Now expand **Entities** and select any entity, for example, **Account**. You will see the relationships listed as shown in the following screenshot:

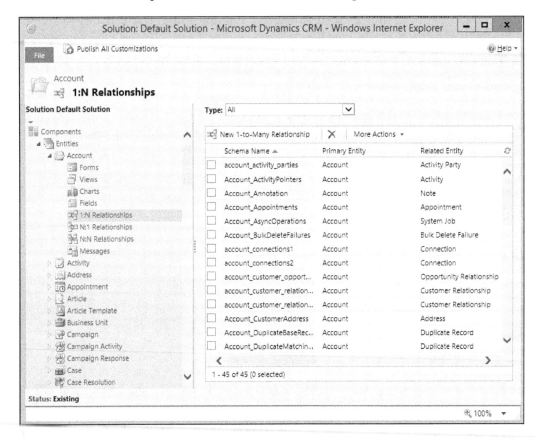

One-to-many relationships (1:N)

These relationships are created when you need to have more than one record of an entity related to a single record of another entity. For example, you can have an account that has more than one contact. In Dynamics CRM, there will be a lookup control in the Contact entity to show the related account, such as the **Parent Customer** field shown in the following screenshot:

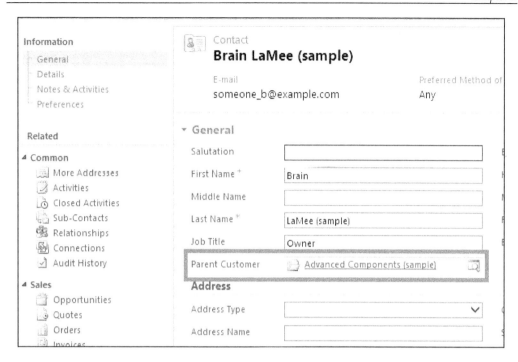

In the **Account** form, there will be a new entry added to the sitemap with the name of **Contacts** to show the related contact entries as shown in the following screenshot:

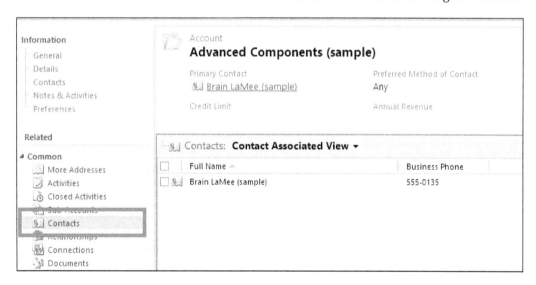

In the **Customization** section of the **Account** entity, you will see these 1:N relationships, and on opening it you will see the following details page:

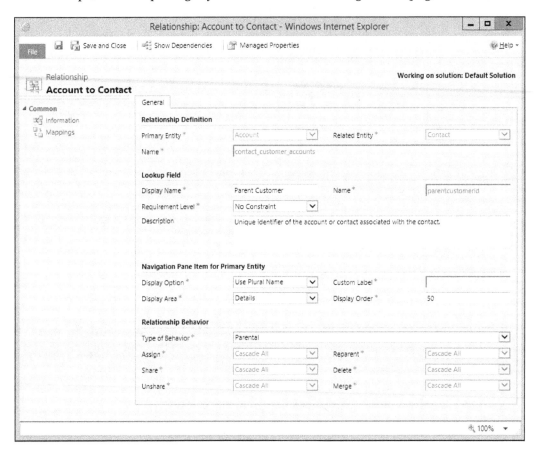

Many-to-one relationships (N:1)

On the other hand, if we are looking at the `Contact` entity, we will see the same relationship we described in the 1:N example, but backwards. So if we open the `Contact` entity and go to the N:1 relationships, we will see the same relation we saw in the `Account` entity under the 1:N relationships.

It is important to know that when we create any type of relationship between two entities, we need to publish both entities for the changes to take effect. Similarly, when we want to export one entity, we will also need to include the related entities in our solution file to replicate the same customization in another organization or environment.

Many-to-many relationships (N:N)

We use this type of relationship when we need to have one record of an entity that needs to be related to more than one record of another entity and at the same time this entity needs to have more than one record related to the first entity. For example, suppose we have a marketing list that can contain more than one account while at the same time an account can belong to more than one marketing list. In Dynamics CRM, this relationship will look as follows:

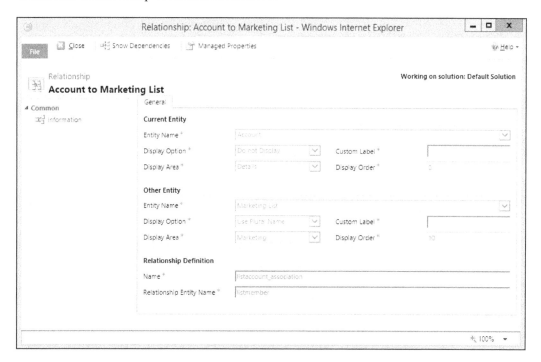

In the **Account** form, there won't be a lookup like in the 1:N relationship, and instead they will be added to the sitemap of both entities. For example, in the Account entity, there will be a node to show the marketing lists and in the marketing lists, there will be a node to show the accounts. In this particular case, they will be shown under the marketing members list. This example shows a particular case of a polymorphic relationship that, at this moment, cannot be created and only exists in the out-of-the-box system.

SQL overview

It is very important to have good knowledge and experience with SQL. **SQL** is short for **Structured Query Language**, and it is commonly used to handle and manage database records. Microsoft SQL Server has its own type of SQL called T-SQL or Transact-SQL. In this chapter we are going to use SQL Management Studio, which is installed along with Microsoft SQL Server.

The main commands of this language are Select, Update, Delete, and Insert.

Select

This command is used to query records from the database.

The syntax used is as follows:

```
Select field1, field2 from table
Select field1, field2 from view
```

We use the filtered views as follows:

```
Select name, address1_stateorprovince from FilteredAccount
```

Downloading the example code

You can download the example code files for all Packt Publishing books you have purchased from your account at http://www.PacktPub.com. If you purchased this book elsewhere, you can visit http://www.PacktPub.com/support and register to have the files e-mailed directly to you.

This will produce the results shown in the following screenshot:

	name	address1_stateorprovince
1	Remoting Coders	NULL
2	A Store (sample)	TX
3	Advanced Components (sample)	TX
4	Affordable Equipment (sample)	TX
5	Basic Company (sample)	TN
6	Best o' Things (sample)	KA
7	Designer Goods (sample)	WA
8	Blue Company (sample)	WA
9	Elemental Goods (sample)	TX
10	Grand Store (sample)	WA
11	Litware Inc. (sample)	CA
12	Magnificent Store (sample)	IN
13	Recreation Supplies (sample)	IN
14	Unusual Store (sample)	MA
15	Variety Store (sample)	NC

In this book we are using the CRM sample data, which you can install by going to **Settings | Data Management | Sample Data | Install Sample Data**. Having the sample data installed will produce very similar results to what are described in the samples.

If you want to get all the fields, you can just use the * char as follows:

```
Select * from table
```

For example, see the following query:

```
Select * from FilteredAccount
```

This will produce the results shown in the following screenshot:

	accountcategorycode	accountcategorycodename	accountclassificationcode	accountclassificationcodename	accountid	accountnu
1	NULL	NULL	1	Default Value	175960B5-781E-E211-93F1-00155DFE080F	NULL
2	NULL	NULL	1	Default Value	9934856A-CA20-E211-93F1-00155DFE080F	ABSS4G4!
3	NULL	NULL	1	Default Value	9B34856A-CA20-E211-93F1-00155DFE080F	ACTBBDC
4	NULL	NULL	1	Default Value	9D34856A-CA20-E211-93F1-00155DFE080F	ABC28UU'
5	NULL	NULL	1	Default Value	9F34856A-CA20-E211-93F1-00155DFE080F	AFFSE9IK
6	NULL	NULL	1	Default Value	A134856A-CA20-E211-93F1-00155DFE080F	ACSHN2S
7	NULL	NULL	1	Default Value	A334856A-CA20-E211-93F1-00155DFE080F	NULL
8	NULL	NULL	1	Default Value	A534856A-CA20-E211-93F1-00155DFE080F	NULL
9	NULL	NULL	1	Default Value	A734856A-CA20-E211-93F1-00155DFE080F	ABCO9M3
10	NULL	NULL	1	Default Value	A934856A-CA20-E211-93F1-00155DFE080F	NULL
11	NULL	NULL	1	Default Value	AB34856A-CA20-E211-93F1-00155DFE080F	BABCO88I
12	NULL	NULL	1	Default Value	AD34856A-CA20-E211-93F1-00155DFE080F	BOBC3J9L
13	NULL	NULL	1	Default Value	AF34856A-CA20-E211-93F1-00155DFE080F	BAK8JYGF
14	NULL	NULL	1	Default Value	B134856A-CA20-E211-93F1-00155DFE080F	BTBS3G34
15	NULL	NULL	1	Default Value	B334856A-CA20-E211-93F1-00155DFE080F	BBA38GH'

If you want to get a number of records only, you need to use the TOP keyword. For example, if we only want to get the first two records, we use the following command:

```
Select TOP 2 name, address1_stateorprovince from FilteredAccount
```

This will produce the results shown in the following screenshot:

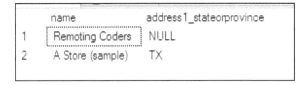

	name	address1_stateorprovince
1	Remoting Coders	NULL
2	A Store (sample)	TX

There are also some text transformation functions you can use in your `select` command; for example, if you want to return all the values of a field in uppercase or in lowercase as shown in the following command:

```
Select UPPER(name), LOWER(address1_stateorprovince) from FilteredAccount
```

This will produce the results shown in the following screenshot:

	(No column name)	(No column name)
1	REMOTING CODERS	NULL
2	A STORE (SAMPLE)	tx
3	ADVANCED COMPONENTS (SAMPLE)	tx
4	AFFORDABLE EQUIPMENT (SAMPLE)	tx
5	BASIC COMPANY (SAMPLE)	tn
6	BEST O' THINGS (SAMPLE)	ka
7	DESIGNER GOODS (SAMPLE)	wa
8	BLUE COMPANY (SAMPLE)	wa
9	ELEMENTAL GOODS (SAMPLE)	tx
10	GRAND STORE (SAMPLE)	wa
11	LITWARE INC. (SAMPLE)	ca
12	MAGNIFICENT STORE (SAMPLE)	in
13	RECREATION SUPPLIES (SAMPLE)	in
14	UNUSUAL STORE (SAMPLE)	ma
15	VARIETY STORE (SAMPLE)	nc

As you can see in the previous screenshot, when using functions, the column names are missing; so we will need to add a column alias as follows:

```
Select UPPER(name) as name , LOWER(address1_stateorprovince) as address1_
stateorprovince from FilteredAccount
```

Notice that you can omit the `as` keyword; the following code will produce the same result:

```
Select UPPER(name) name , LOWER(address1_stateorprovince) address1_
stateorprovince from FilteredAccount
```

 Even though you can apply text transformations in your SQL query, it might not be recommended to do that here because, as we will see later in this book, you will also be able to apply text transformations on your report.

Update

The Update command is used to edit the data stored in the database. The syntax is as follows:

```
Update table set field = value, field = value
```

Notice that if you don't specify a WHERE condition, all the records will be updated; for example, the following command will update the country field with the U.S. value to all records in the Account table:

```
Update FilteredAccount set address1_country = 'U.S.'
```

> It is not recommended to perform the Update, Delete, and Insert operations on the CRM database from SQL directly as it is an unsupported method. When you need to perform these operations, always use the web services so the plugins and workflows that might be associated with those operations can be fired.

Delete

The Delete command removes records from the database. The basic command is as follows:

```
Delete from table
```

Note that when using this command, if you don't specify a WHERE condition, it will delete all the records; be careful and use a WHERE clause when using this command, as follows:

```
Delete from table where field = value
```

Insert

The Insert command adds records to a table. The syntax is as follows:

```
INSERT INTO tablename (field1, field2) VALUES (value1, value2)
```

Have in mind that inserting records to the CRM tables is not an easy task because it requires inserting records in at least two different tables. We should never insert records into the CRM tables manually with SQL code; however, we will find the Insert command useful when working with temporary tables, as you will see later in this chapter in the *SQL advanced* section.

WHERE

Most of the time we want to filter the query results in such a way that they return a set of records but not all the records that exist in the table; this is when we use the WHERE clause.

```
Select * from FilteredAccount WHERE name = 'damian'
```

You can also use the AND operator to filter by another column as follows:

```
Select * from FilteredAccount WHERE name = 'damian' AND telephone1 =
'9999'
```

With the AND operator, both name and phone number need to match the returned records. If you want to filter by a field or another field, we use the OR operator as follows:

```
Select * from FilteredAccount WHERE name = 'damian' OR telephone1 =
'9999'
```

If you want to filter by a part of a string, similar to the contains operator in the **Advanced Find**, you use the like operator with the % character at the beginning and the end of the string; for example:

```
Select * from FilteredAccount WHERE name like '%damian%'
```

This will return records with account names such as the following:

```
Damian
Mr Damian Sinay
Damian Sinay
Mr Damian
```

If you want to filter by a string that begins with another string, use the like operator with the % character at the beginning of the string; for example:

```
Select * from FilteredAccount WHERE name like '%damian'
```

This will return records with account names such as the following:

```
damian
Mr Damian
```

If you want to filter by a string that ends with another string, use the like operator with the % character at the end of the string; for example:

```
Select * from FilteredAccount WHERE name like 'damian%'
```

This will return records with account names such as the following:

```
damian
Damian Sinay
```

ORDER BY

To sort the results, we use the ORDER BY clause; for example:

```
Select name from FilteredAccount ORDER BY name asc
```

This command will generate the results shown in the following screenshot:

By default, the order will be ascending, so we can omit the word asc at the end, as shown in the following code, and yet it will generate the same result:

```
Select * from FilteredAccount ORDER BY name
```

To get the results in the descending order, we change asc by desc as shown in the following command:

```
Select * from FilteredAccount ORDER BY name desc
```

This sentence will generate the results shown in the following screenshot:

	name
1	Variety Store (sample)
2	Unusual Store (sample)
3	Remoting Coders
4	Recreation Supplies (sample)
5	Magnificent Store (sample)
6	Litware Inc. (sample)
7	Grand Store (sample)
8	Elemental Goods (sample)
9	Designer Goods (sample)
10	Blue Company (sample)
11	Best o' Things (sample)
12	Basic Company (sample)
13	Affordable Equipment (sample)
14	Advanced Components (sample)
15	A Store (sample)

group by

To group records, we use the group by statement. There is an important consideration when using this statement; the fields we select will also need to be included in the group by statement, and if not included we will need to use one of the following aggregate functions:

- AVG
- MIN
- CHECKSUM_AGG
- SUM
- COUNT
- STDEV
- COUNT_BIG
- STDEVP
- GROUPING
- VAR
- GROUPING_ID
- VARP
- MAX

An example of this is as follows:

```
Select address1_stateorprovince from FilteredAccount group by address1_
stateorprovince
```

This will produce the results shown in the following screenshot:

	address1_stateorprovince
1	NULL
2	CA
3	IN
4	KA
5	MA
6	NC
7	TN
8	TX
9	WA

Using the aggregate functions, we can show how many records of each state are there, as follows:

```
Select address1_stateorprovince, count(*) from FilteredAccount  group
by address1_stateorprovince
```

This will produce the results shown in the following screenshot:

	address1_stateorprovince	(No column name)
1	NULL	1
2	CA	1
3	IN	2
4	KA	1
5	MA	1
6	NC	1
7	TN	1
8	TX	4
9	WA	3

As we can see, the column that shows the number of records per state doesn't have a name, so it will be good to name this column using an alias, as follows:

```
Select address1_stateorprovince, count(*) as state_count from
FilteredAccount  group by address1_stateorprovince
```

The keyword `as` can be omitted; the following code will have the same result:

```
Select address1_stateorprovince, count(*) state_count from
FilteredAccount  group by address1_stateorprovince
```

We can now see the result with the `state_count` name on the second column as shown in the following screenshot:

	address1_stateorprovince	state_count
1	NULL	1
2	CA	1
3	IN	2
4	KA	1
5	MA	1
6	NC	1
7	TN	1
8	TX	4
9	WA	3

join

Sometimes we want to show fields from different tables. This is when we need to use the `join` clause. Notice that there need not be a relationship between the tables to join them in a SQL command, but the performance will be better if they are related. For example, suppose we want to show the name of the contacts as well as the name of the parent account; in this case, we can use a query as follows:

```
Select FilteredContact.fullname, FilteredAccount.name   from
FilteredContact inner join FilteredAccount on FilteredContact.accountid =
FilteredAccount.accountid
```

This query will produce the results shown in the following screenshot:

	fullname	name
1	Damian Sinay	Remoting Coders
2	Adrian Dumitrascu (sample)	A Store (sample)
3	Brain LaMee (sample)	Advanced Components (sample)
4	Cat Francis (sample)	Affordable Equipment (sample)
5	Cathan Cook (sample)	Basic Company (sample)
6	Darren Parker (sample)	Best o' Things (sample)
7	Eva Corets (sample)	Designer Goods (sample)
8	Forrest Chand (sample)	Blue Company (sample)
9	Gabriele Cannata (sample)	Elemental Goods (sample)
10	George Sullivan (sample)	Grand Store (sample)
11	Marco Tanara (sample)	Litware Inc. (sample)
12	Patrick Steiner (sample)	Magnificent Store (sample)
13	Susan Burk (sample)	Recreation Supplies (sample)
14	Thomas Axen (sample)	Unusual Store (sample)
15	Yvonne McKay (sample)	Variety Store (sample)

The same query can be written in a shorter manner by using table aliases as follows:

```
select C.fullname, A.name from FilteredContact C inner join
FilteredAccount A on C.accountid = A.accountid
```

It is best practice to use table aliases when using the `join` clause.

SQL advanced

We are now going to see some advanced functions of the SQL language, which we might need to use on complex queries or reports. Creating or dropping temporary or static tables, using and executing stored procedures, managing cursors, and working with transactions are some of the advanced SQL queries we will look at in the following sections.

CREATE TABLE

There might be cases when you might want to create temporary tables; they are especially useful when using cursors.

The command to create a table is as follows:

```
CREATE TABLE tablename (
Fieldname type,
Fieldname type)
```

For example, the following code will create a customer's table with two fields:

```
CREATE TABLE customers(
   name varchar(100),
   age int
)
```

To create temporary tables, we usually add a # character to the name of the table; for example:

```
CREATE TABLE #customers(
   name varchar(100),
   age int
)
```

DROP TABLE

After you are done with the temporary table you created, it is a good practice to remove the table from the system. The command to delete a table is the DROP TABLE command; the following is an example:

```
DROP TABLE #temptable
```

Stored procedures

A stored procedure is a very good way to store our queries in a way that we can use them more than once; SQL Server will optimize the execution by precompiling the query, so the next time we call the stored procedure, it will run faster.

To create a stored procedure you use the CREATE command as follows:

```
CREATE PROCEDURE mySP
AS
BEGIN
  SET NOCOUNT ON;
    -- Insert statements for procedure here
  SELECT * from FilteredAccount
END
```

To modify a stored procedure we use the ALTER command as follows:

```
ALTER PROCEDURE mySP
AS
BEGIN
  SET NOCOUNT ON;
    -- Insert statements for procedure here
  SELECT name from FilteredAccount
END
```

To delete a stored procedure we use the DROP command as follows:

```
DROP PROCEDURE mySP
```

To execute a stored procedure we use the EXEC command as follows:

```
EXEC mySP
```

Notice that you will be able to use stored procedures only in CRM on-premise environments as the CRM online and partner hosted environments will not give you access to the database to create a stored procedure or use SQL data sources. Have in mind when using store procedures that it is not a supported way to place them in the same database as the CRM organization database. You can, however, store them on a separated database in the same SQL Server pointing to the CRM organization database. This is to allow the CRM to check the referential integrity when upgrading the database on the rollup updates. For more information refer to http://msdn.microsoft.com/en-us/library/gg328350.aspx.

Cursors

Cursors are used when you need to read row by row from a query that generates more than one row in its result. If you need to make a calculation, for example, to show subtotals then you might need to use cursors.

To use a cursor you will first need to declare it as follows:

```
DECLARE account_cursor CURSOR FOR Select name, revenue from
FilteredAccount
```

After you declare the cursor you will need to open it to start the calculation:

```
OPEN account_cursor
```

We will need to declare one variable per field. We will retrieve the value of the fields from the query we used in the cursor. In our example, we will need a variable to store the name and another to store the revenue, so we declare the variables as follows:

```
declare @name as varchar(160)
declare @revenue as money
```

We are now ready to fetch the rows one-by-one:

```
FETCH NEXT FROM account_cursor INTO @name, @revenue
WHILE @@FETCH_STATUS = 0
BEGIN
  -- do something here
  print @name  + ' ' + CAST( isnull(@revenue, '') as varchar(40))
  FETCH NEXT FROM account_cursor INTO @name, @revenue
END
```

Notice that in the code we will first use the FECTH NEXT method that will retrieve the first row and assign the values into the @name and @revenue variables; we will then iterate on the rest of the records by looking at the @@FETCH_STATUS flag. It will be equal to zero if there are more records available to read; otherwise it will be distinct to zero and our loop will be completed.

Between the BEGIN and END lines and before the last FECTH flag is where we put our logic, as shown in the following screenshot. In our example we are just printing the values.

```
Messages
   Remoting Coders 0.00
   A Store (sample) 0.00
   Advanced Components (sample) 0.00
   Affordable Equipment (sample) 0.00
   Basic Company (sample) 0.00
   Best o' Things (sample) 0.00
   Designer Goods (sample) 0.00
   Blue Company (sample) 0.00
   Elemental Goods (sample) 0.00
   Grand Store (sample) 0.00
   Litware Inc. (sample) 0.00
   Magnificent Store (sample) 0.00
   Recreation Supplies (sample) 0.00
   Unusual Store (sample) 0.00
   Variety Store (sample) 0.00
```

When you are done with the cursor, you will need to close it and free the memory resources as follows:

```
CLOSE account_cursor
DEALLOCATE account_cursor
```

The complete cursor code will look as follows:

```
DECLARE account_cursor CURSOR FOR Select name, revenue from
FilteredAccount
OPEN account_cursor
declare @name as varchar(160)
declare @revenue as money
FETCH NEXT FROM account_cursor INTO @name, @revenue
WHILE @@FETCH_STATUS = 0
BEGIN
  -- do something here
  print @name  + ' ' + CAST( isnull(@revenue, '') as varchar(40))
  FETCH NEXT FROM account_cursor INTO @name, @revenue
END
CLOSE account_cursor
DEALLOCATE account_cursor
```

Notice that using cursors slows performance; you will need to always think of a way to create your query in a way that you can avoid them.

Transactions

Transactions are used when you need to perform more than one operation such as `Insert`, `Update`, or `Delete` or when you want to validate that the result is what it is expected to be. If everything is good, you commit the transaction; if something goes wrong, you can roll back the transaction and everything goes back to what it was before.

To start a transaction, use the following command:

```
Begin tran T1
```

Here, `T1` is the name of the transaction and can be any name you want. If everything is good with the operations and you want to commit the transaction, you use the following command:

```
Commit tran T1
```

If you want to cancel the transaction and go back to what it was before, you use the following command:

```
Rollback tran T1
```

FetchXML overview

FetchXML is a proprietary query language initially introduced in Dynamics CRM 3.0 and improved through the following versions. All the dynamics CRM views are created with this query language and we can now write reports in CRM 2011 using this query language as well.

The addition of this type of data source allows Dynamics CRM online to create reports where this is the only type of data source supported for CRM Online.

 The FetchXML queries have a limitation of 5000 records per page, so you need to have this in mind when working with them. If you are in CRM on-premise, you can tune this value by touching the registry, setting a value (1) of the `TurnOffFetchThrottling` DWORD key under `HKLM\Software\Microsoft\MSCRM`. For more information, refer to `http://support.microsoft.com/kb/911510`.

The best way to learn how to create a FetchXML query is by using the **Advanced Find** tool.

With this tool, you can easily create queries from where you can download the generated Fetch XML by clicking on the **Download Fetch XML** button.

Notice that this tool won't generate all types of queries (which we can generate manually with XML, such as grouping to create summary results, as we will see later on in this chapter).

 If you are more familiar with SQL sentences, there is an online tool available that converts SQL queries into Fetch XML queries, available at `http://www.sql2fetchxml.com/`.

A sample Fetch XML is as follows:

```
<fetch version="1.0" output-format="xml-platform" mapping="logical"
distinct="false">
  <entity name="account">
    <attribute name="name" />
    <attribute name="primarycontactid" />
    <attribute name="telephone1" />
    <attribute name="accountid" />
    <order attribute="name" descending="false" />
  </entity>
</fetch>
```

Every Fetch XML starts with a root node called `fetch`.

 The full schema of the Fetch XML can be found at `http://msdn.microsoft.com/en-us/library/gg309405.aspx`.

The first child is always the entity node where we specify the primary entity of our query.

To test the Fetch XML queries, we can download the CRM 2011 Fetch XML Execute Tool from CodePlex, which is located at `http://crm2011fetchexecute.codeplex.com/`.

When running this tool, we will need to enter the connection information as follows:

Both the **Discovery Uri** and **Organization Uri** URLs are the URLs we can find when we go to the CRM web interface and then go to **Settings | customizations | Developer resources**.

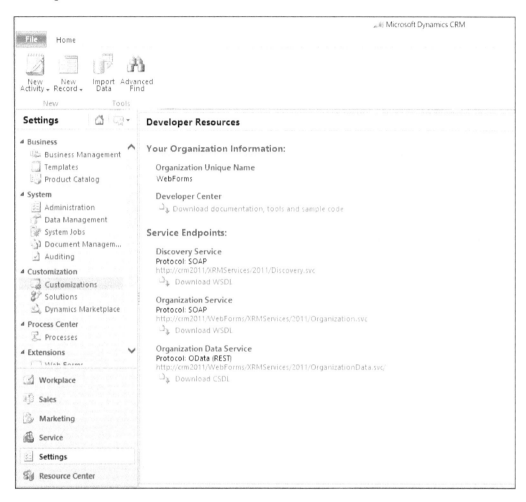

If you want to start writing a Fetch XML query manually, I suggest using the XML editor of Visual Studio; bind the fetch.xsd schema file that comes with the Dynamics CRM 2011 SDK, which can be downloaded from http://www.microsoft.com/en-us/download/details.aspx?id=24004; fetch.xsd is located in the \sdk\schemas folder. Binding the schema will add IntelliSense into our XML editor to avoid misspellings when writing our Fetch XML queries.

If you don't know how to do that, the following is a step by step guide:

1. Open Visual Studio (it can be 2010 or 2012).

2. Go to **File** | **New** | **File...**.

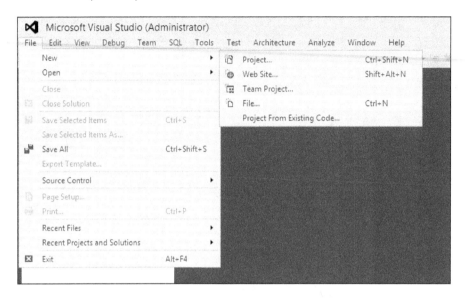

3. Select **XML File** and click on **Open**.

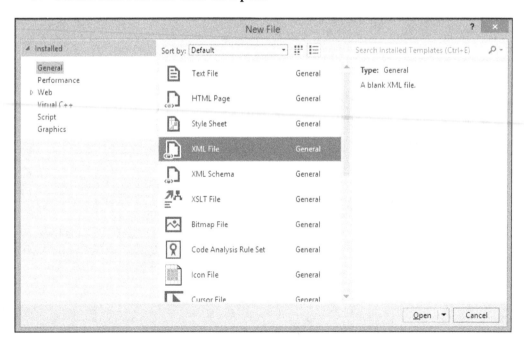

4. Go to the **View** menu and then click on the **Properties** window or hit the *F4* key, as shown in the following screenshot:

5. In the **Properties** window, find the **Schemas** attribute and click on the **...** button, as shown in the following screenshot:

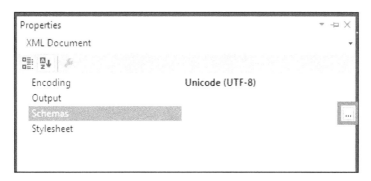

6. In the **XML Schemas** dialog, click on **Add**.

7. Find the `fetch.xml` file in the `crm sdk\schemas` folder as shown in the following screenshot:

8. Click on **OK**.

9. Now you will see full IntelliSense in your XML editor to write FETCH XML queries.

Select fields

To select fields, you add nodes of type `attribute`. For example, to return
the `telephone1` field of the `account` entity, we can write the following code:

```
<fetch version="1.0" mapping="logical" distinct="false">
  <entity name="account">
    <attribute name="telephone1" />
  </entity>
</fetch>
```

The following screenshot shows the selected field:

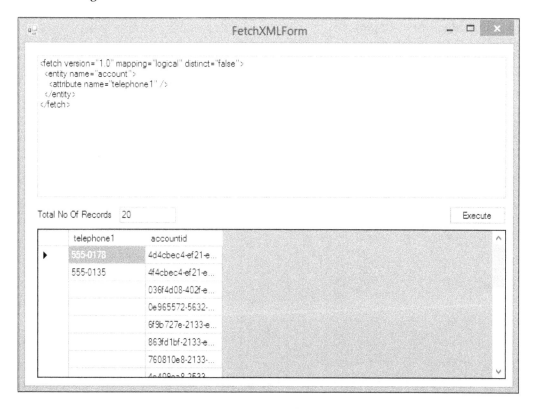

 Notice the primary key field – in this case, the `accountid` field –
will always be returned, so we don't need to add an attribute node
for it.

To return more than one field, we just add more attribute nodes as follows:

```
<fetch version="1.0" mapping="logical" distinct="false">
  <entity name="account">
    <attribute name="telephone1" />
    <attribute name="name" />
  </entity>
</fetch>
```

Here is something you can do with Fetch XML that cannot be generated with the **Advanced Find** tool; it is equivalent to a `select * from entity` query in SQL.

To return all the fields of an entity, you can just pass the `<all-attributes/>` node; the following is an example:

```
<fetch distinct='false' mapping='logical'>
  <entity name='account'>
    <all-attributes/>
  </entity>
</fetch>
```

We will see the result as follows:

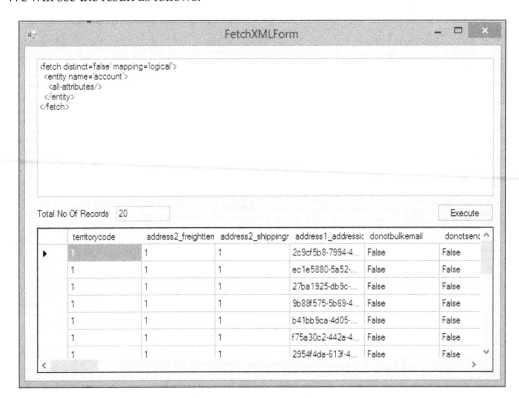

Filters and conditions

To filter, you add nodes of type `filter` and specify the AND or OR operator in the `type` attribute. Filters are equivalent to the WHERE clause in SQL.

The following is an example:

```
<fetch version="1.0" output-format="xml-platform" mapping="logical"
distinct="false">
  <entity name="account">
    <attribute name-"telcphone1" />
    <filter type="and">
      <condition attribute="name" operator="eq" value="Remoting
Coders" />
    </filter>
  </entity>
</fetch>
```

In this example, we query the Account entity and return the `telephone1` field by filtering the `account name` field that needs to be equal to a value.

The operators available to use are as follows:

- `eq` (equal)
- `like` (contains)
- `not-like` (does not contain)
- `ne` (not equal)
- `null` (does not contain data)
- `not-null` (contains data)

The following are examples of commands using these operators:

- To filter by a field that is equal to a value, we use the following command:

  ```
  <condition attribute="name" operator="eq" value="Remoting" />
  ```

- To filter by a field that contains a value, we use the following command:

  ```
  <condition attribute="name" operator="like" value="%Remoting%" />
  ```

- To filter by a field that starts with another string, we use the following command:

  ```
  <condition attribute="name" operator="like" value="Remoting%" />
  ```

- To filter by a field that ends with a part of a string, we use the following command:

```
<condition attribute="name" operator="like" value="%Remoting" />
```

- To filter by a field that is not equal to a value, we use the following command:

```
<condition attribute="name" operator="ne" value="Remoting" />
```

- To filter by a field that contains data, we use the following command:

```
<condition attribute="name" operator="not-null" />
```

- To filter by a field that does not contain data, we use the following command:

```
<condition attribute="name" operator="null" />
```

Order by

To order a field, you add a node of type `order` and specify the field you want to order in the attribute and the direction in the descending order of attributes; the following example will return the `name` and `telephone1` fields of the `account` entity in the ascending order of the name field:

```
<fetch version="1.0" output-format="xml-platform" mapping="logical"
distinct="false">
  <entity name="account">
    <attribute name="name" />
    <attribute name="telephone1" />
    <order attribute="name" descending="false" />
  </entity>
</fetch>
```

To sort in the opposite order, you just change the descending attribute to `true` as follows:

```
<order attribute="name" descending="true" />
```

If you want to order by more than one field, you just add another order node as follows:

```
<order attribute="name" descending="true" />
<order attribute="telephone1" descending="false" />
```

This previous code will sort first by name in descending order and then by `telephone1` in ascending order.

Group by

To group, you add the `aggregate='true'` attribute to the `fetch` node.

Just as in SQL, when using the `group by` option, you will need to either return the fields that are grouped or use aggregated functions for the other fields. The aggregated functions that are supported are as follows:

- `sum`
- `avg`
- `min`
- `max`
- `count`

Further, examples of grouping the accounts by the `name` field to return the count of records with different names are as follows:

```
<fetch distinct='false' mapping='logical' aggregate='true'>
  <entity name='account'>
    <attribute name='name' aggregate='count' alias='counter'/>
  </entity>
</fetch>
```

Testing this code will give us the following result:

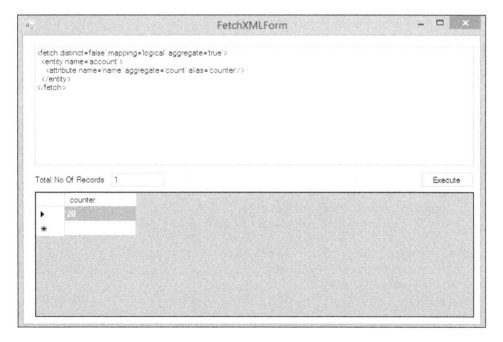

Linking to other entities

If you want to get the fields of one related entity, you will need to use the `link-entity` node and specify the join type. There are two types of joins supported by Fetch XML:

- Inner join
- Outer join

Inner join

The inner join will only show records of the primary entity that has a related record. For example, in the following code, we will return all the accounts that have a primary contact associated and will return the full name of the contact:

```
<fetch version="1.0" output-format="xml-platform" mapping="logical"
distinct="false">
  <entity name="account">
    <attribute name="name" />
    <attribute name="telephone1" />
    <order attribute="name" descending="false" />
    <link-entity name="contact" from="contactid" to="primarycontactid"
visible="false" alias="praccount">
      <attribute name="fullname" />
    </link-entity>
  </entity>
</fetch>
```

Outer join

Contrary to an inner join, the outer join returns records that do not depend on the secondary entity records. To use outer join, change the link-type attribute to `outer` as follows:

```
<fetch version="1.0" output-format="xml-platform" mapping="logical"
distinct="false">
  <entity name="account">
    <attribute name="name" />
    <attribute name="telephone1" />
    <order attribute="name" descending="false" />
    <link-entity name="contact" from="contactid" to="primarycontactid"
visible="false" link-type="outer" alias=" praccount">
      <attribute name="fullname" />
    </link-entity>
  </entity>
</fetch>
```

This example will return accounts regardless of the `primary contact` value, meaning that if there is no primary contact for that account, the record will be returned in the result with null value in the `primary contact` field.

Summary

In this chapter we have explained the entity relationship model of Dynamics CRM and reviewed the basic and advanced commands of the SQL language as well as the FetchXML language that we will need to use in order to create the queries we will use on our reports. We are going to keep using these two languages in the following chapters.

In the next chapter we will be creating our first report using the Report wizard and we will be exporting the report to be edited using Visual Studio 2008.

3
Creating Your First Report in CRM

In this chapter, we are going to create our first Microsoft Dynamics CRM 2011 report, for which we are going to use the following tools:

- Using Microsoft Dynamics CRM 2011 Report Wizard
- Using Visual Studio
- Publishing the report

Using Microsoft Dynamics CRM 2011 Report Wizard

The Report Wizard is the easiest way to create a report; with this tool any person without any knowledge of development can create a simple report. Of course, the reports that are being created with the Report Wizard will have some limitations, but for more than one purpose they might be enough.

The reports created with this wizard will have the benefits of the export tool that is included in the SSRS Report Control that allows us to export the report to XML, CSV, PDF, MSHTML, Excel, TIFF, and Word formats.

Any report created with the Report Wizard can also be modified with the same Report Wizard. The Report Wizard allows you to filter what entities and fields you want to display, and also gives the ability to prefilter the records when running the report to give more flexibility to the results.

To create a new report, follow the given steps:

1. Navigate to **Workplace**.
2. In the Navigation Pane, click on **Reports**.
3. Click on **New**.

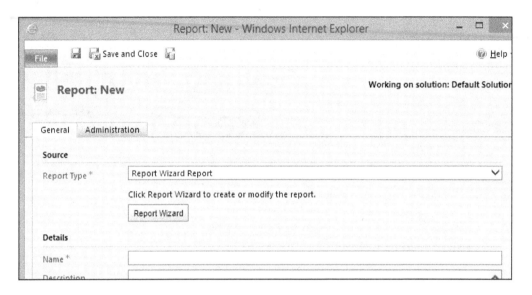

 All the fields in the window shown in the previous screenshot were already explained in *Chapter 1, Introduction to Reporting in Microsoft Dynamics CRM*; refer to that chapter for more details about the fields in this window.

4. Click on the **Report Wizard** button to start the wizard that will allow you to create a report.

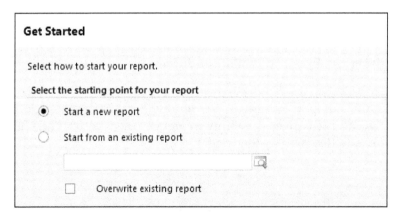

In the first screen you will be presented with two options: the first option will allow you to create a new report, while the second option will allow you to start from an existing report. Notice that you will be able to use the second option only for any existing report that was previously created with the Report Wizard.

5. For our first report, we will keep the first option selected and click on the **Next** button.

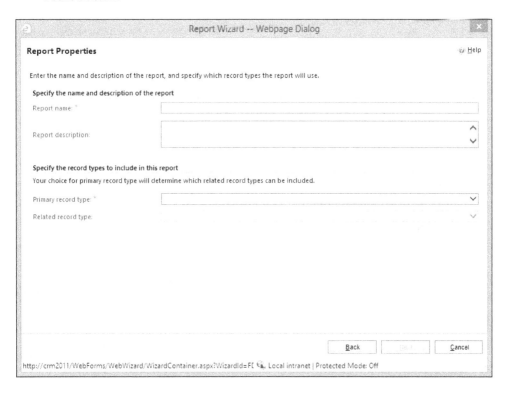

There are two mandatory fields that you need to fill: **Report name**, which is the name of the report so that you can easily find it later, and the **Primary record type**, which is the primary entity where the report will display the result. You can optionally enter the **Report description** and the **Related record type**; this is one limitation of the Report Wizard that it only allows you to select one single related record type.

6. For this example, we will enter the name `First report wizard for account` and select the **Accounts** entity as the **Primary record type**, as shown in the following screenshot:

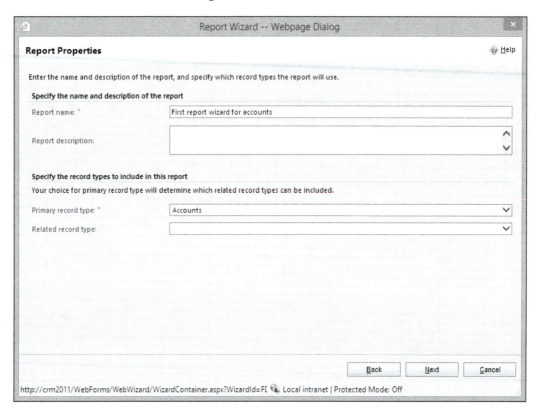

For the primary record type, you can specify any entity that is available in the system, including the custom entities you create. The related record type will depend on the relationships that the primary entity you selected has. For example, you could create a report for the Report entity that would show all the reports that are created in the CRM 2011 organization. Or, you could also create a report to show the processes (such as workflows or dialogs) that were run at a specific period of time.

7. Click on **Next** to continue to the next step where the filters will be presented.

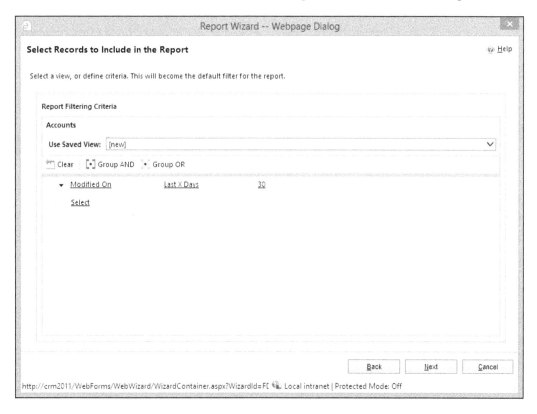

On this screen, you can add the filter criteria you want to use for the report; you can select one of the saved views or system views, or start from a new query. The interface is similar to the **Advanced Find** tool.

The filter criteria you select here can also be changed when running the report. This is what is called the default report filter criteria, which you can also change alone without having to rerun the wizard by just going to **Reports**, selecting a report, and clicking on the **Edit Default Filter** button that is on the ribbon.

8. We will select the **Active Accounts** system view for this example and click on **Next** to continue.

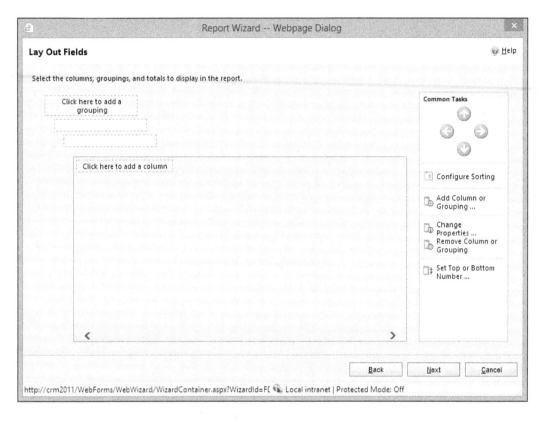

9. In this window, you select the fields you want to be displayed on the report; you have three different types of groups to use and then fill in the details in the main box. Clicking on the main box where it says **Click here to add a column** will allow you to select the columns; for this example, we will select the **Account Name** field as follows:

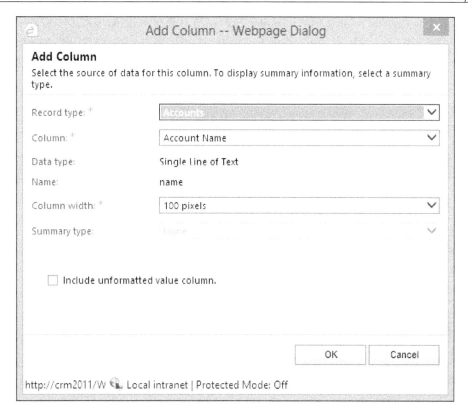

We can also change the width of the columns here or select the column and clicking on **Change Properties**; the options we can use to set the width of the columns are limited to 25px, 50px, 75px, 100px, 125px, 150px, 200px, and 300px.

In this dialog box, you will see the option **Include unformatted value column**. This option is not enabled for every field, but is only enabled for fields where the types are Date Only, Date and Time, Whole Number, Decimal, Currency, or Floating Point Number. The purpose of this option is to allow the field to be handled in an Excel file when the report is exported to that format, as by default, if you do not select this option, all the fields will be exported with the string format causing some problems when you want to use calculations in Excel.

10. Click on **OK** to add the field. We will repeat this process to add the **Address 1: City**, **Address 1: State/Province**, and **Address 1: Country/Region** fields so the details should look as shown in the following screenshot:

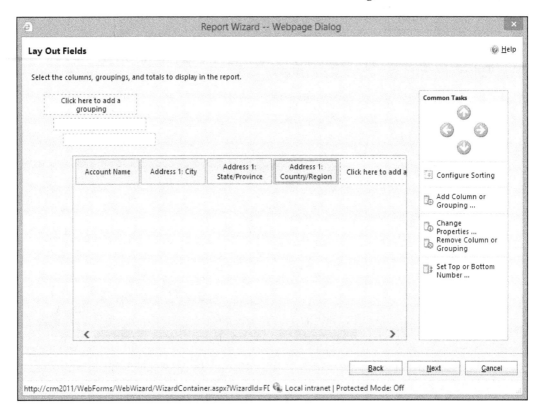

11. We won't add a grouping for now, but we will set the way we want the record to be sorted by clicking on the **Configure Sorting** option.

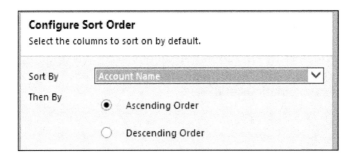

Configuring the sorting will allow us to sort only by the fields we added to the details of the report as well as set the direction to ascending or descending.

12. For this example, we will order by **Account Name**; so, select this field and click on **OK**.

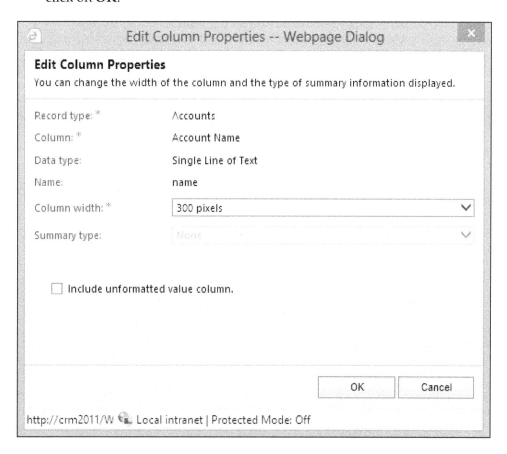

13. For this sample we will change the **Account Name** field to **300 pixels** and click on **OK**. Then click on **Next** in the main Report Wizard screen.

The **Summary type** option will only be enabled for fields of type number, decimal, floating point, and currency, and will show the options we can use on aggregation such as Average, Maximum, Minimum, Percent of total, and Sum.

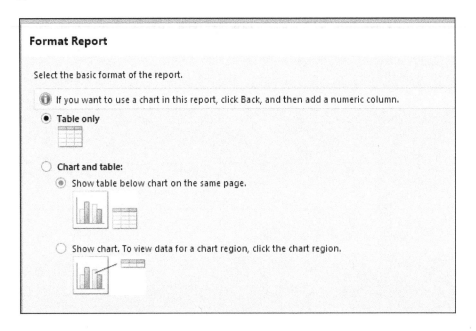

14. On this screen, we have two main options of report types we can create with this wizard: **Table only** and **Chart and table**. For this first report, we will choose **Table only** and click on **Next**. The options to select **Chart and table** might be disabled, and that is because we need to select a numeric type field on our report in order to use the charts, as we can see in the warning displayed in yellow in the previous screenshot.

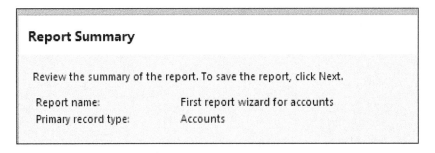

15. We are now presented with a summary of the report that we are about to create. Click on **Next** to continue.

16. After the report is created, the last screen will show you the status of the report. In this case it was successfully created, so we can click on **Finish** to close the wizard.

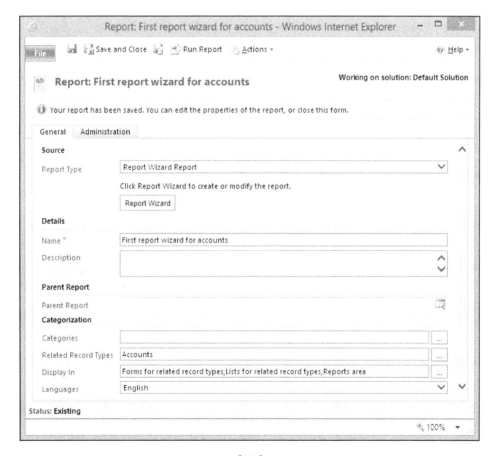

Once the report is created, we will be taken back to the first screen where we initiated the Report Wizard, but this time with the **Related Record Types**, **Display in**, and **Languages** fields completed; we now have the option to assign a category if we want. We can also click on **Run Report** to see how our new report looks.

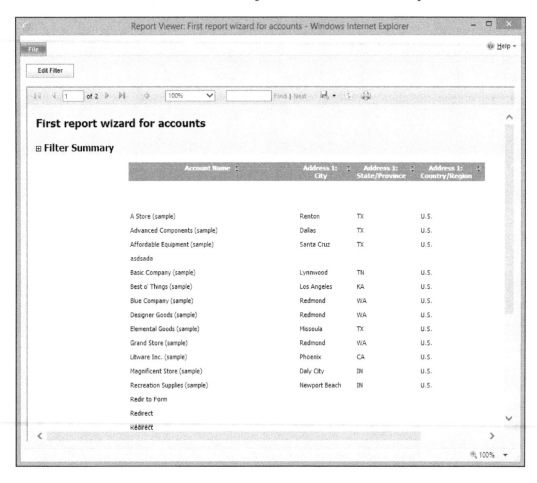

As with any other report, this report is displayed using the SSRS Report Control that allows us to export the report to XML, CSV, PDF, MSHTML, Excel, TIFF, and Word formats.

The Report Wizard will also make the columns sortable by default, so clicking on any column will change the order and direction.

In the header of the report, we will have the **Filter Summary**. When we expand it by clicking on the plus icon, it will show information about the prefilters used when we ran the report. In our case, by default it will show **Accounts: Modified On: Last X Days 30**.

first report wizard for accounts

⊟ Filter Summary

Accounts:
  Modified On: Last X Days 30

We can also add grouping fields; for example, adding the **Address 1: State/Province** field to the report result created with the CRM Report Wizard would look like the following:

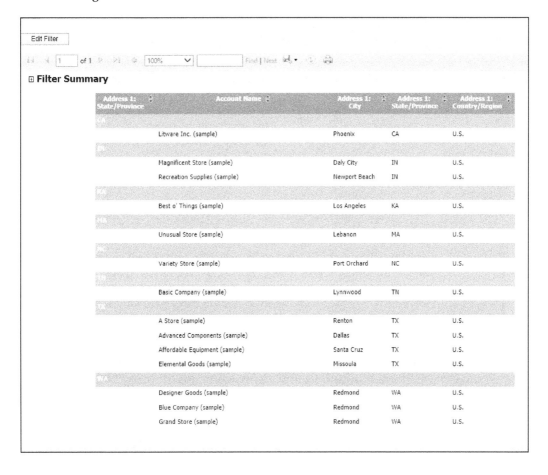

Using Visual Studio

The best recommendation before starting to create a report with Visual Studio is to create a report with the Report Wizard first and then export the RDL file generated by the Report Wizard to import on a Visual Studio project. By going to the **Actions** menu of the report you created and clicking on **Download Report**, you can download the RDL file.

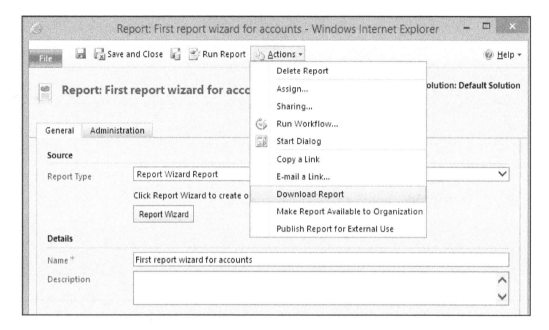

The **Make Report Available to Organization** option that appears under **Download Report** will do the same thing as we change the **Viewable By** option to **Organization** on the **Administration** tab. If the report is already set to **Viewable By Organization**, this option will change to **Revert to Personal Report**, which will be the same as setting the **Viewable By** option to **Individual** from the **Administration** tab.

Now you can start Visual Studio 2008 and create a new report project by performing the following steps:

1. Navigate to **File | New | Project...** as shown in the following screenshot:

2. Select the **Report Server Project** template that is on the **Business Intelligence** group.

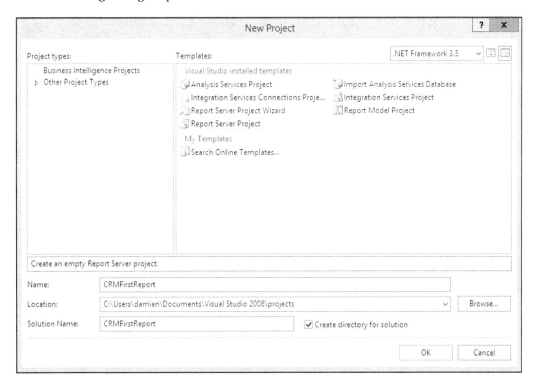

3. Enter the name for your project and click on **OK**.

4. In the Solution Explorer window, right click on **Reports** and navigate to **Add | Existing Item...** as follows:

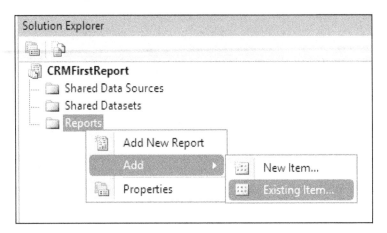

5. Select the file you downloaded earlier and click on **Add**.

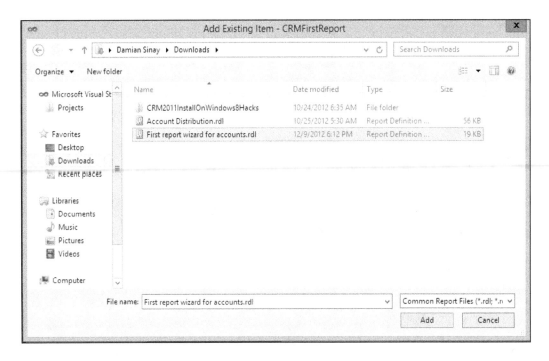

You should now see your report in the `Reports` folder as shown in the following screenshot:

6. Double-click on the report name to open the report, and under the **Report Data** window that will be displayed on the left-hand side of the window, expand **Data Sources** and select **CRM** as shown in the following screenshot:

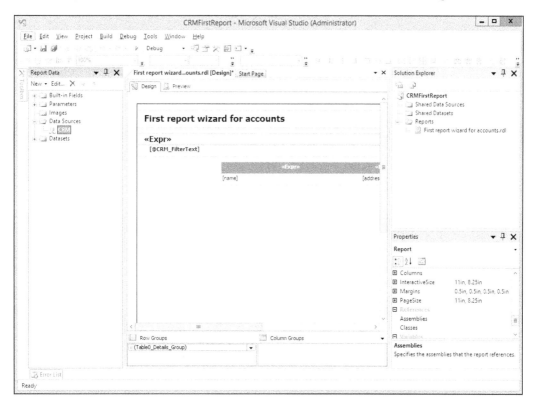

7. Double-click on **CRM Data Source** to configure your connection.

 If you don't see the **Report Data** window, you can go to the **View** menu and select the **Report Data** option or press *Ctrl + Alt + D*.

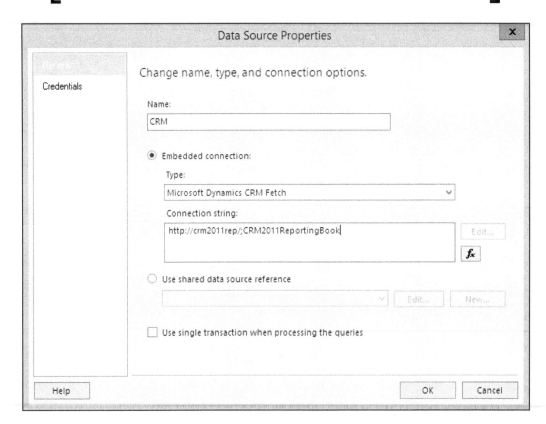

You will notice that the **Type** selected for the **Embedded connection** is **Microsoft Dynamics CRM Fetch**; if you don't see this type, it is because you didn't install the CRM Reporting Authoring Extensions as we have explained in the first chapter of this book.

The connection string will show the CRM Server URL separated by a semicolon with the organization name. For example, `http://crm2011rep/;CRM2011Repo rtingBook`, where the server name is `CRM2011rep` and the organization name is `CRM2011ReportingBook`.

To verify the connection or build your data set, expand **Datasets** from **Report Data** and select the **DSMain** dataset as shown in the following screenshot:

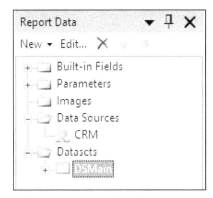

8. Double-click on **DSMain** to open the **Dataset Properties** window.

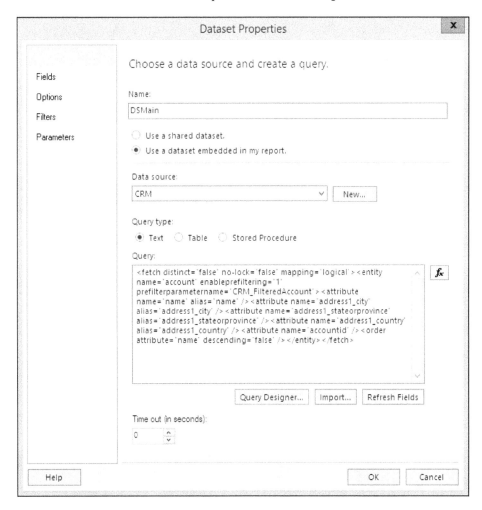

9. Click on **Query Designer** to verify the connection with Dynamics CRM.

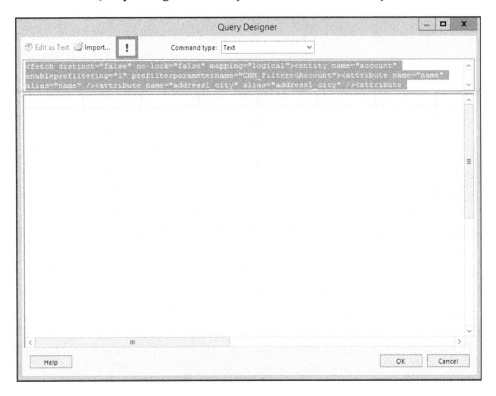

In this window, you can change the Fetch XML query and test the results by clicking on the red explanatory button, where you will be able to see the records returned by your query.

If you are prompted by the **Define Query Parameters** dialog box, you can leave the null value for the **CRM_FilteredAccount** parameter as shown in the following screenshot:

The parameters such as **CRM_FilteredAccount** are a good way to make more flexible queries that will allow the user to modify the query results by using the prefilters when running the report without having to ask the report developer if he wants, for example, to see different results for active or inactive accounts. Leaving a value null will mean we don't want to use a prefilter and we want to return all the account records.

10. Click on **OK** to see the results.

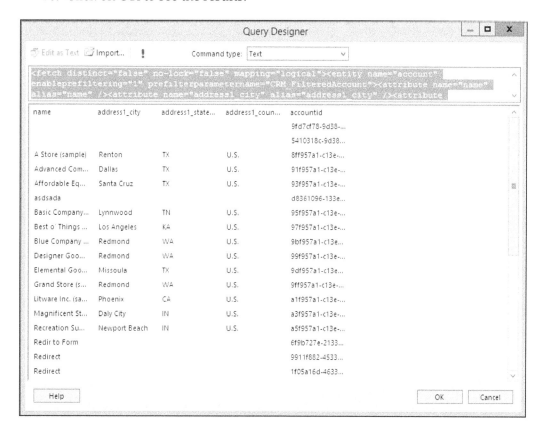

We can now click on **OK** to close **Query Designer** and then click on **OK** to close the **Dataset Properties** window.

We are now going to make a change on this report that we could not make with the Report Wizard. For example, changing the background color of the report to light green and changing the font size of the title to a higher value.

1. To change the background color of the report, select the report and go to the **Properties** window. Be sure you are in the **Body** control and find the **BackgroundColor** property and select the light green color as shown in the following screenshot:

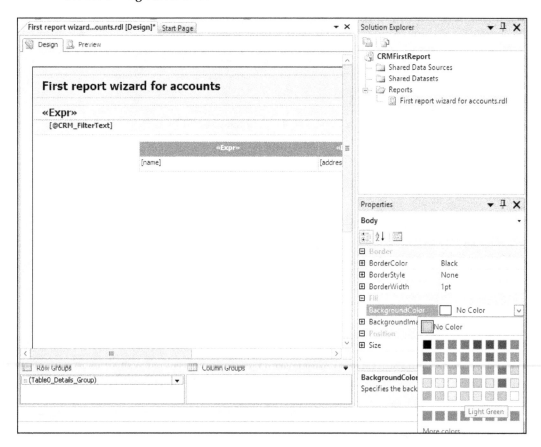

2. To change the font size of the title, select the title and go to the **Properties** window. Be sure you have the **txtHeader** control selected, then find the **FontSize** property and change the value to 20pt as shown in the following screenshot:

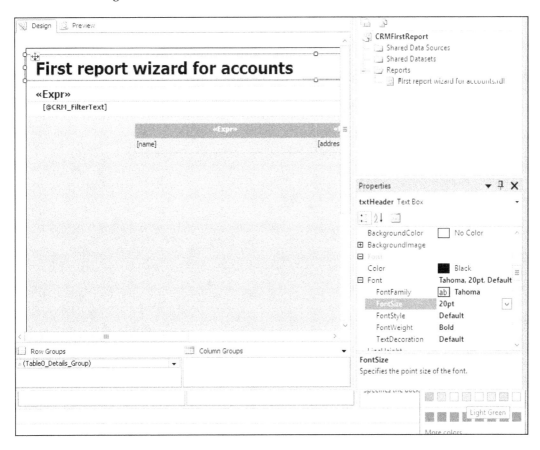

3. You can see how the report looks like by clicking on the **Preview** tab that is near the **Design** tab, which is the default tab of the report. This will allow you to troubleshoot and preview your report before uploading it to Dynamics CRM.

4. We can now save the report and upload it to CRM; to do that, we need to go to the CRM web interface and edit the report. When the edit window is open, change **Report Type** to **Existing File** and enter data in the the **File Location** field of the report using the report path of the report we edited in Visual Studio.

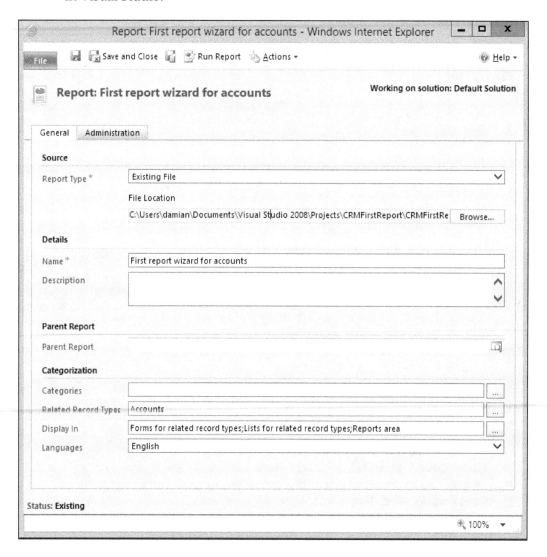

5. Click on **Save** and then on **Run Report** to see the results.

6. If you are prompted with the following dialog box, click on **OK** to continue:

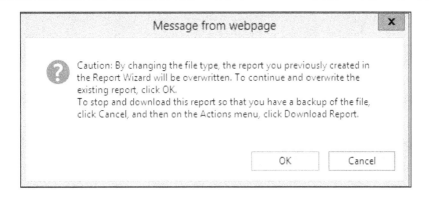

As the dialog box states, every report that is created with the CRM 2011 Report Wizard can be easily modified using the same Report Wizard unless it is touched by Visual Studio, for example; in that case you won't be able to modify it again using the CRM 2011 Report Wizard, and the only option to modify the report will be by using Visual Studio or the Report Builder, as we will see in the next chapter.

Publishing the report

The reports we created with the Report Wizard or the ones we created with Visual Studio and then uploaded to CRM are not going to be visible if we go to the Reporting Service Manager interface. By default, all the reports are hidden, and if we want to make one of them visible, we need to publish it.

To publish a report, we go to the **Actions** menu then select **Publish Report for External Use,** as shown in the following screenshot:

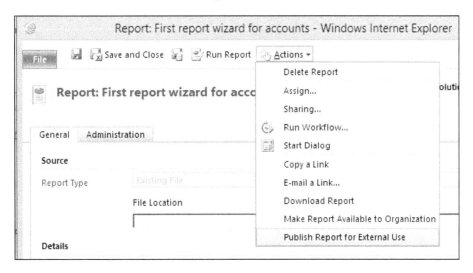

Summary

In this chapter, we have created our first report using the Report Wizard and we also exported the report to be edited with Visual Studio 2008, where we made some customizations to re-upload the report to Dynamics CRM. We have also seen how to publish the report to be visible on the Reporting Server manager for external use.

In the next chapter, we will create our first report using the Report Builder and we will also see the features we can use that were not available in the standard CRM Report Wizard.

4
SQL Server Report Builder

In this chapter, we are going to create reports using SQL Server Report Builder. This is a tool that comes with SQL Server Reporting Services, as we will see in this chapter, and is more powerful than the CRM Report Wizard we saw in the previous chapter. It will help us create better reports without using Visual Studio.

This is a tool designed for intermediate users, and it allows us to include images, drawing controls such as lines and squares, charts, geographic maps, and it allows us to change the text font styles.

In this chapter we are going to cover the following topics:

- Report Builder versions
- Report Builder limitations

Report Builder overview

Report Builder is a tool that is available for download directly from the Report Manager interface of SQL Reporting Services; if we don't know the Report Manager URL, we can check it in SQL's **Reporting Services Configuration Manager** as shown in the following screenshot. This tool is located where SQL Reporting Services is installed in the server.

We will be working with Version 3.0, which is the same version that comes with SQL Server 2008 R2 as well as SQL Server 2012.

We can also download the standalone version of Report Builder from the Microsoft website (if you don't have access to the SQL Server Manager interface) by going to `http://www.microsoft.com/en-us/download/details.aspx?id=6116` to download the 2008 version or by going to `http://www.microsoft.com/en-us/download/details.aspx?id=35576` to download the 2012 with SP1 version.

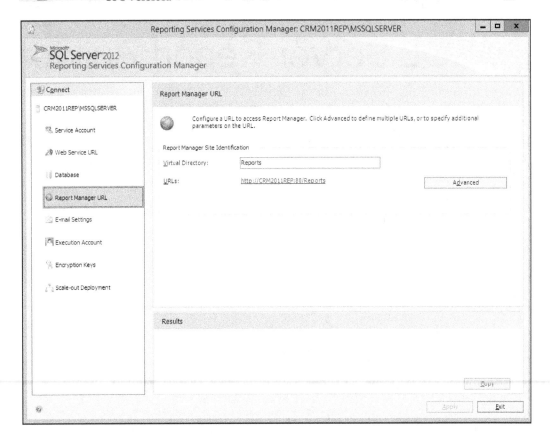

When we click on **Report Manager URL**, we will see the following interface open:

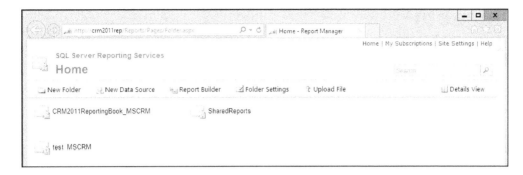

Clicking on the **Report Builder** menu option that is located in the top menu bar will download and install Report Builder on our machine.

Once we have Report Builder installed on our computer, the first screen we will see is the **Getting Started** window.

In order to create a report, the first thing we need to do is create a new dataset, as the reports generated by Report Builder can only use the datasets created with this tool.

Datasets

There are two types of datasets: shared and embedded. To create a shared dataset, we will need to have access to SQL Reporting Services, as the shared dataset will be stored there to be accessible for future reports. If we don't have access to the SQL Server Reporting Services, we can skip this step and create an embedded dataset that will be embedded within our report (RDL file).

To create a new shared dataset, follow the ensuing steps:

1. Click on **New Dataset**.

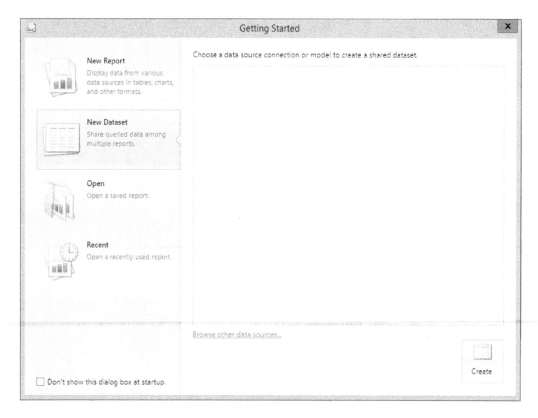

2. Click on the **Browse other data sources** link and find the **MSCRM_ DataSource** data source for our organization; it will usually be located in a folder with our organization name plus the _MSCRM suffix, for example, CRMORG_MSCRM. These are shared data sources that were created by the CRM Setup application when the CRM was initially deployed.

If we are using the standalone version of Report Builder, we won't be able to create or browse shared data sources.

There are also two main types of data sources: embedded and shared. The shared ones are stored in the SQL Server Reporting Services, while the embedded ones will store the data source connection details inside the RDL report file.

CRM 2011 installs two shared data sources per CRM organization by default. One uses the SQL Server connection type while the other one uses Fetch XML.

3. Select **MSCRM_DataSource** and click on **Open**.

4. Click on **Create** to go to the **Dataset Editor** window.

   This window is the one that will allow us to design our query; from here, we will be able to see the database schema objects, such as tables, views, and functions. We will be able to select the object we want to use on our query as well as preview the results to validate the query.

The database view panel will show two main folders for the CRM shared data source:

- ○ dbo

- ○ MetadataSchema

The dbo folder will show the objects related to the organization entities, such as the account, contacts, and lead.

The MetadataSchema folder will show CRM schema entities, such as the attributes, relationships, and the entities themselves, which might be useful if we want to create a report that will display the number of custom entities installed on our CRM organization.

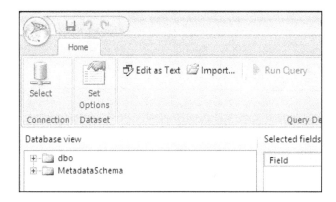

5. Expand the **dbo** folder and then expand the **Views** folder as follows to locate the views.

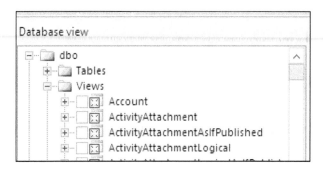

6. Select the **FilteredAccount** view as shown in the next screenshot:

As we already explained in the previous chapters, filtered views are good for maintaining the security constraints of the records, so they will only return the records that the user, who runs the report, has read permissions for.

7. We will see all the fields displayed in the **Selected fields** list. We can add filters if we want to show only a partial view of the records by clicking on the following icon .

8. This will add a new record inside the **Applied filters** list; we can add a filter to show only the active accounts by using the **statuscode** field, the value of which is set to **1,** as shown in the following screenshot:

9. To see the results, we can click on the **Run Query** button that is on the ribbon.

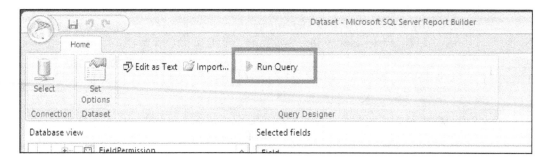

This will show us a preview of the records returned by the query inside the **Query results** panel, which appears at the bottom of the screen.

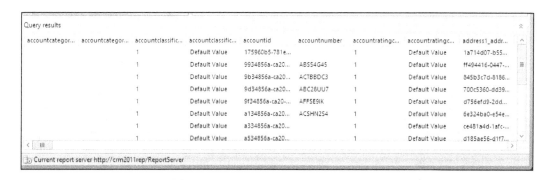

If we want to limit the number of columns returned by the query, we can expand the **FilteredAccount** view and uncheck the fields we don't want returned. Selecting only the necessary fields will improve the performance of our report. For example, we can select only the **accountid**, **accountnumber**, **name**, and **createdon** fields.

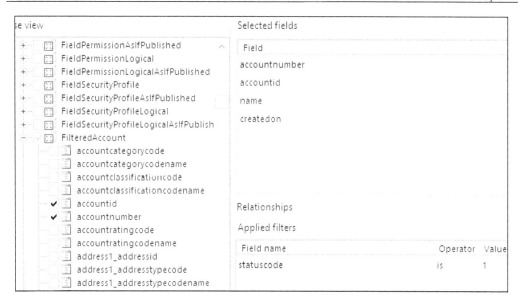

We can also change the order in which the file will be returned by a query by using the up and down arrows that are on the right-hand side of the **Selected fields** list header.

If we want to use a custom entity on our report, the filtered view will be named with the schema name prefixed by the publisher prefix that, by default, is set to **New_,** so a custom entity called Houses will likely have a view named **FilteredNew_Houses,** for example.

Query Designer

Clicking on the **Edit as Text** button located in the ribbon will give us the ability to use a standard SQL editor that will give us better flexibility if we are more familiar with this language.

We can also import an SQL file if we created it before using SQL Management Studio; clicking on the **Import** button will allow us to load an SQL file that we can choose from our local disks.

When working in the text mode, we will be able to preview the results by clicking on the red exclamation mark (!). The results will be displayed in the bottom part of the window.

In the applied filters list, we can mark the **Parameter** checkbox to make a field we used on the filters a parameter.

The operator types we can use in the filters are as follows:

- like / not like
- is / is not
- is any of
- is none of
- is more than
- is less than / is more than
- is less than or equal to / is more than or equal to

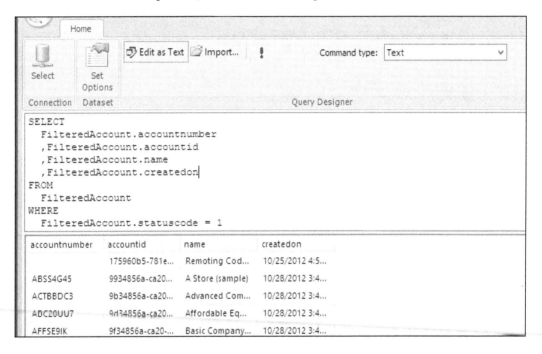

This mode will also give us the ability to change the **Command Type** listbox to use a stored procedure.

To save the dataset, click on the **Save** icon that is located in the window near the top-left border.

We will be asked to enter a name for our dataset and a location inside the report server where we want this to be stored.

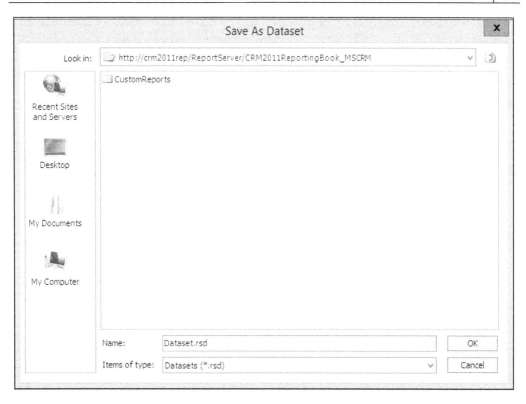

For this first demo purpose, I will select the CRM organization folder and leave the default `DataSet1.rsd` name, and then click on **OK** to continue.

Creating a new report

Now that we have our shared dataset created, we can close the dataset designer and open Report Builder again to select the option to create a new report.

The options available to create a new report are:

- **Table or Matrix Wizard**
- **Chart Wizard**
- **Map Wizard**
- **Blank Report**

We will see that the list of the available report types we can create is very similar to the one exposed by the CRM Report Wizard we saw in *Chapter 3, Creating your first Report in CRM*, with the exception of the Map Wizard, which we will show later.

The **Blank Report** option would be a good option for advanced users who won't need to start from a wizard, letting us decide what controls and layout we want to use.

Table or Matrix Wizard

Since this is the first report we will create with Report Builder, we will use **Table or Matrix Wizard**.

If you have downloaded a report from CRM, you can select the **Open** option.

Going to the **Recent** section will show us the latest report we designed for the server we are connected to.

Chart Wizard will allow us to select from any of the following chart types:

- Column
- Line
- Bar
- Area

Select the **Choose an existing dataset in this report or a shared dataset** option, locate the dataset we created before, and click on **Next**.

If you don't see the dataset listed here, click on **Browse** to add a shared dataset to this list.

In this screen, we will see four main listboxes:

- **Available fields**
- **Rows Groups**
- **Column Groups**
- **$\sum$ Values**

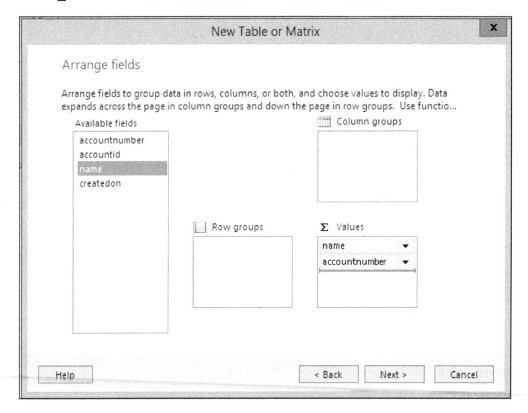

We can drag-and-drop the fields from the **Available fields** lists to any of the three listboxes displayed. If we want to create a group or row group, or if we want to only show the fields in the details, we can drag-and-drop to the values list.

To delete a field from any of these lists, select the field and hit the *Delete* key on our keyboard, as there is no delete button or contextual menu option.

Note that adding a field to the value or groups won't remove the field from the available fields, as we can add them more than once to the values or groups.

We can also add an aggregation on any field by clicking on the arrow near the field; this will especially be useful if we add fields on the **Row groups** or **Column Groups** listboxes.

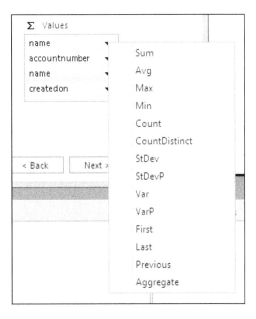

The available aggregation functions we can select are:

- **Sum**: This can only be used with numeric fields and returns the sum of all the values
- **Avg**: This returns the average of the values
- **Max** and **Min**: These return the maximum or minimum value
- **Count**: This returns the count of the records
- **ContDistinct**: This returns the count of the records with different values
- **StDev**: This returns the statistical standard deviation of all values
- **StDevP**: This returns the statistical standard deviation for the population for all values
- **Var**: This returns the statistical variance of all values
- **VarP**: This returns the statistical variance for the population for all values
- **First** and **Last**: These return the first or last value
- **Previous**: This returns the previous value in the specific scope
- **Aggregate**: This returns a custom aggregate of the specified expression as defined by the data provider

For this first report, we won't use any aggregation and will simply click on **Next**.

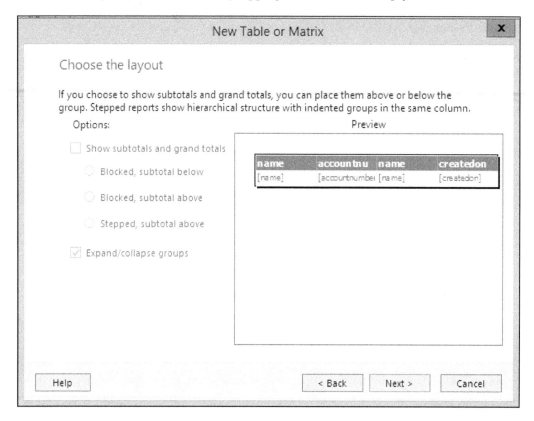

Note that the **Show subtotals and grand totals** options are disabled here because we didn't select any field of the type number or currency, or didn't use any aggregation type such as **Count** or **Sum**.

The different options we can select to show the subtotals are:

- **Blocked, subtotal below**: This specifies whether the subtotals should be displayed below the group

- **Blocked, subtotal above**: This specifies whether the subtotals should be displayed above the group

- **Stepped, subtotal above**: This specifies whether the report should show a hierarchical structure with the indented groups in the same column

By default, the option **Expand/collapse groups** will be checked.

Clicking on **Next** will allow us to select a style.

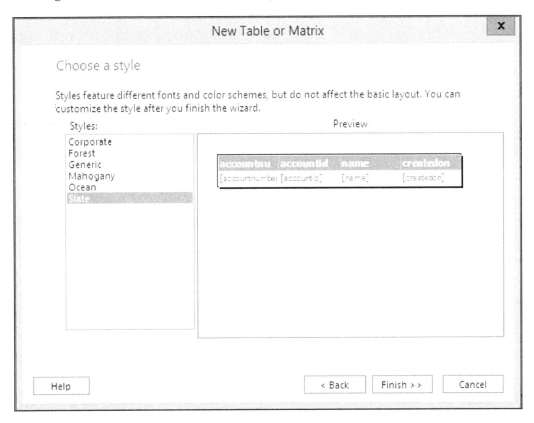

We can only select from one of the six predefined styles, which can be any of the following:

- Corporate
- Forest
- Generic
- Mahogany
- Ocean
- State

Each of these styles differ from the font style used as well as the column header's background color used.

Now let's select the style we want and click on **Finish**.

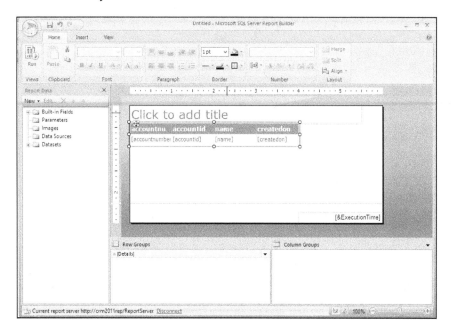

We can click on the **Run** button that is on the ribbon to test our report.

Our report should look as follows:

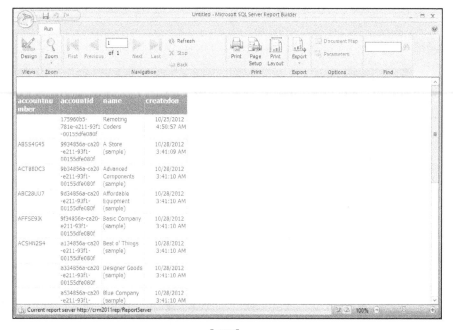

We can easily add a title to the report by clicking on the **Click to add title** textbox that is already created by the wizard and located at the top of the table. The execution time will also be included on the footer by default.

Running the report will also allow us to do all the things we can usually do when viewing a report with the report viewer, such as exporting the report to different formats (Microsoft Excel, Microsoft Word, PDF, and so on). Print and preview the report.

Running the report for the first time might be a little slow if it is the first time we are connecting to the SQL Reporting Service; we are going to look at and explain some performance improvement techniques later in *Chapter 9*, *Failure Recovery and Best Practices*.

Click on the **Design** button to go back to the report designer.

We can easily add sorting to the column headers by following the given steps:

1. Let's select the column header where we want to add the sorting.
2. Right-click on the column header textbox and select **Text Box Properties...** as shown in the following screenshot:

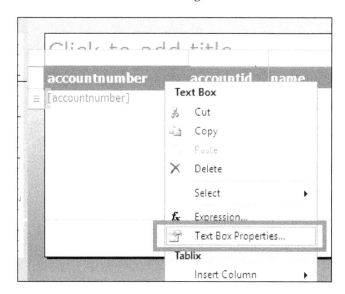

3. In the **Text Box Properties...** dialog, go to the **Interactive Sorting** tab and check the checkbox that says **Enable interactive sorting on this text box**; then, select the **[accountnumber]** field in the **Sort by** drop-down list as shown in the following screenshot:

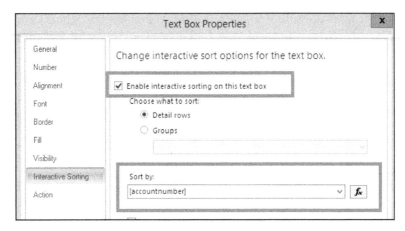

This will allow us to select which field we want to use when sorting the column if we used a different name on the column header.

4. Click on **OK** to close the **Text Box Properties...** dialog.

If we now run the report, we will see a little icon near the column header that when clicked on, will sort the column as shown in the following screenshot:

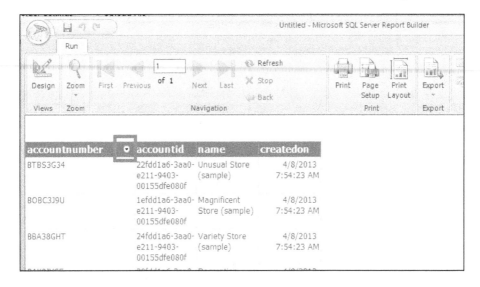

Inside each textbox that is included in the table, we can also add custom actions to make the values link to other reports or bookmarks, or even go to an external URL.

Refer to the section *Working with control events*, *Appendix*, *Expression Snippets*. for more details on how to use custom actions.

> To create a bookmark, enter a name on the bookmark property of any textbox control.

Adding a logo to our report

Now we can do something cool with the report that we cannot do with the CRM Report Wizard. Before the addition of this tool, it was only possible to do certain things with Visual Studio. Something as simple and as necessary as adding the logo of our company to the header can be done easily with this tool. To add a logo to the report, follow the ensuing steps:

1. Click on the **Insert** tab and then on the **Image** button that is inside the **Report Items** group on the ribbon.

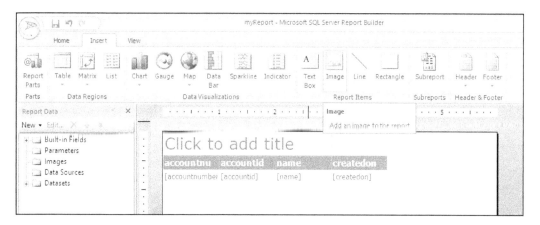

2. Using the mouse, we can select the location where we want to place the image on the report, and as soon as we release the mouse button, we will be presented with the following dialog box:

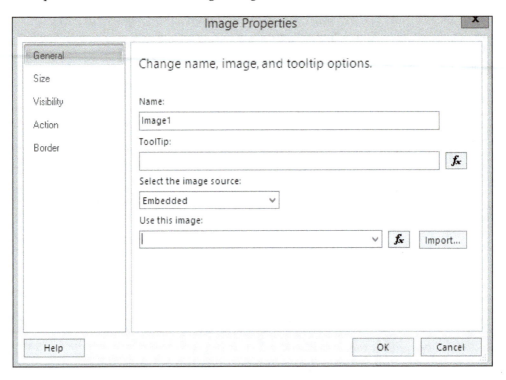

The types of images we can use are:

- ○ GIF
- ○ JPG
- ○ PMG
- ○ BMP

3. Note that we can also add lines and rectangles that can be filled by a color or an image. We'll click on the **Import** button to select the image from our local disk and folders.

We must enter a name for the image and optionally a tooltip that we wish to display when the user moves the mouse over the image. We can use expressions on the tooltip and image; refer to *Chapter 5, Creating Contextual Reports,* for a better description of expressions or *Appendix, Expression Snippets,* for more references.

The **Visibility** tab will allow us to configure when we want the image to be displayed, which can also be displayed using an expression if we want to depend on a specific field value.

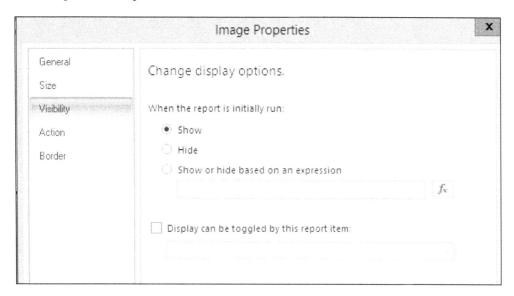

4. The **Action** tab will allow us to add a link on the image to allow the user to navigate to another report, bookmark, or go to an external URL.

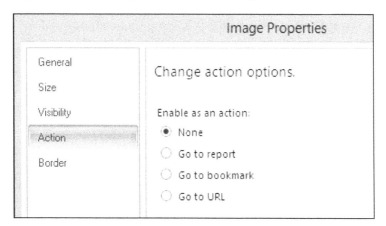

5. The **Border** tab will also allow us to use expressions on the border's style and width.

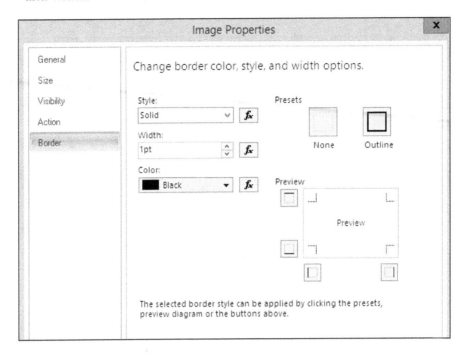

6. Click on **OK** to close the **Image Properties** dialog; the report with the image should look similar to the following screenshot:

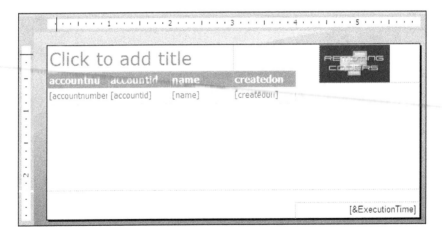

We can use three different image source types:

- ° **Embedded**: This is the source type we used that allows us to select a file from our local machine, and it will be encoded and saved within the RDL file

- ° **External**: This option will allow us to use an image file located in the Report Server

- ° **Database**: This option will allow us to select a database field where we'll have the binary representation of the image if we have an image database

7. Let's click on **Save** to save our report. Similarly to what we did for the dataset, we will need to specify the report server folder and a name for the report; note that the report extension is still an RDL file, so it can be edited in Visual Studio if we want. We can also import the report in Dynamics CRM 2011 web interface by creating a new report and selecting the option of using an existing file. In this case, we will probably want to use some of CRM's predefined parameters; refer to *Chapter 5, Creating Contextual Reports,* for more details on the CRM parameters.

We can also add indicators to the reports, which are under **Data Visualizations**, to show the different icons that can be displayed in different colors or styles depending on the specific field value we configure. This is another alternative to use predefined configurable images, such as directional arrows, symbols, and shapes, such as bubbles or rating, to show X number of starts, depending on an associated field value.

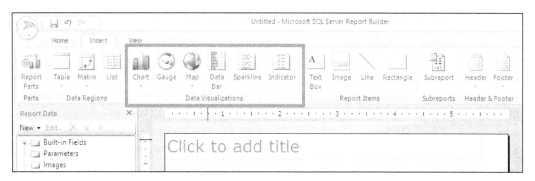

The **Indicator** control comes with a very neat gallery of icons that will save us a lot of time, as they are commonly used on any report or document. These are good alternatives to images, so we can consider them before re-inventing the wheel by using custom image controls with expressions.

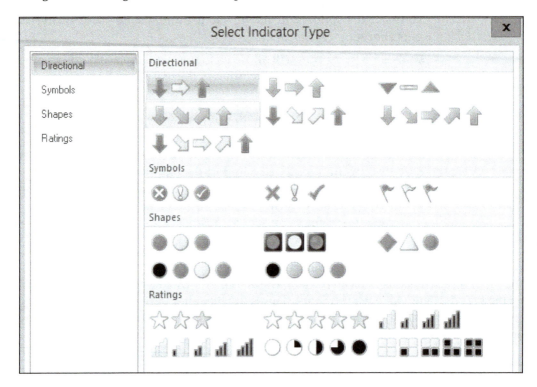

Advanced reports with Report Builder

We are now going to look at some of the advanced report types we can create with the Report Builder tool, such as creating a report to show geographic maps. To create a Map report, we will need to create a dataset with at least one field that contains the address of a state; for example, if we wanted to show the accounts on a map by state, we would create a dataset as follows:

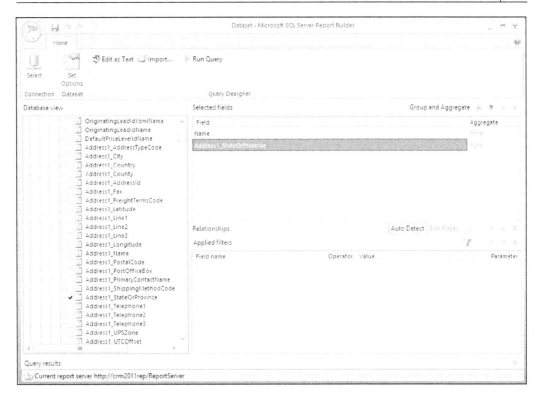

Save the new dataset with a name such as `AccountByStateDataset`. Close Report Builder and open it again. To create a new Map report, select the **Map Wizard** option when the **Getting Started** window is presented.

Map Wizard

The following dialog box allows us to use one of the predefined maps that are available; they are as follows:

- **Map gallery**
- **ESRI shapefile**
- **SQL Server spatial query**

Inside the Map gallery, we can select one of the following options for USA:

- **States by County**
- **USA by State**
- **USA by State Exploded**
- **USA by State Inset**

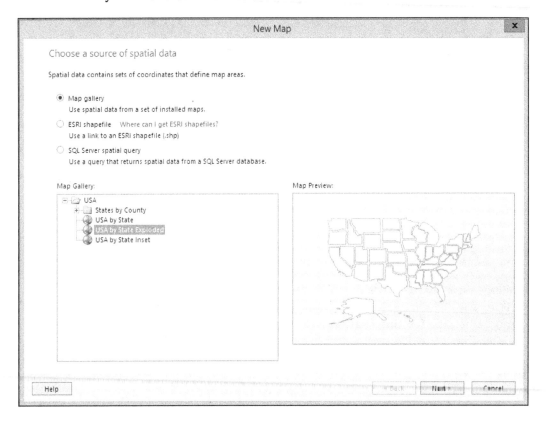

The **ESRI shapefile** and **SQL Server spatial query** options will let us use custom map types.

The quickest way is to use one of the three predefined options that are included in the gallery, such as the **USA by State Exploded** option.

 Only the U.S. maps are available in the gallery, so if we want to create a report for another country, we will have to get the maps from the **ESRI shapefile** link.

Click on **Next** to continue.

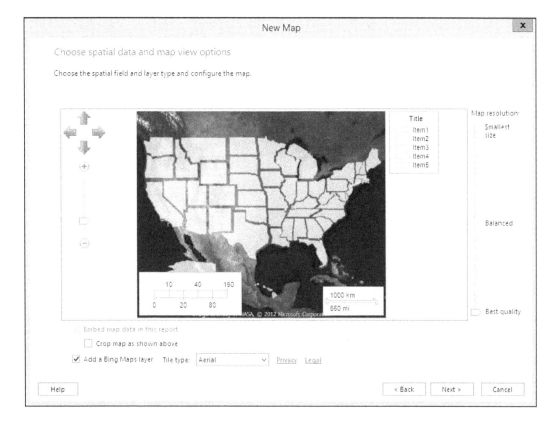

On this screen, we can add Bing Maps Layers; the options for adding them are:

- **Road**
- **Aerial**
- **Hybrid**

We can zoom in to the map to start in the state we want and also change the map position.

We can also change the map resolution from **Smallest size** for better performance to **Best quality** for better graphics.

Be sure to check the privacy and legal policies when using this type of report, as they might change in the future because they link to the external Microsoft public website.

Click on **Next** to continue.

Map visualization types

Here we can select one of the three map visualizations. The options we can select are:

- **Basic Map**
- **Color Analytical Map**
- **Bubble Map**

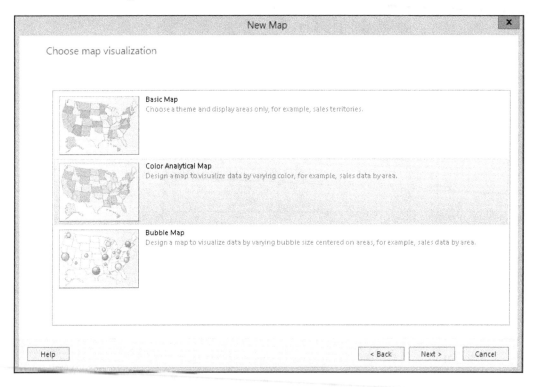

The **Basic Map** option allows us to select a single color map.

For this example, we will select the **Color Analytical Map** option and click on **Next** to continue.

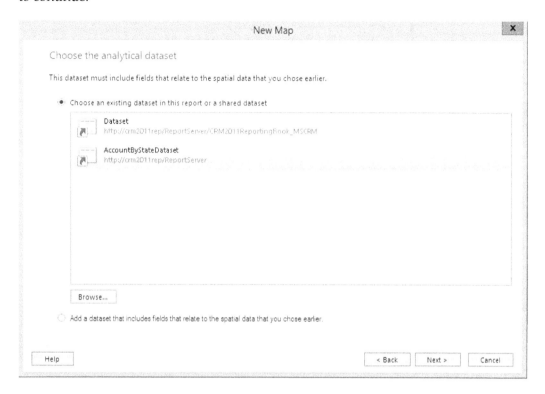

Let's select the dataset we created before; note that if we don't find it on the list, we need to click on the **Browse** button, navigate to the folder location where we stored the dataset, and select it. If we didn't create it before or want to use another one, we can also create a new one from this screen. Click on **Next** to continue.

This screen will ask us to select the field that matches the states from the fields we included in our dataset. We need to be sure that we have included at least one field with the U.S. state information or geographic information (such as latitude and longitude) in our dataset.

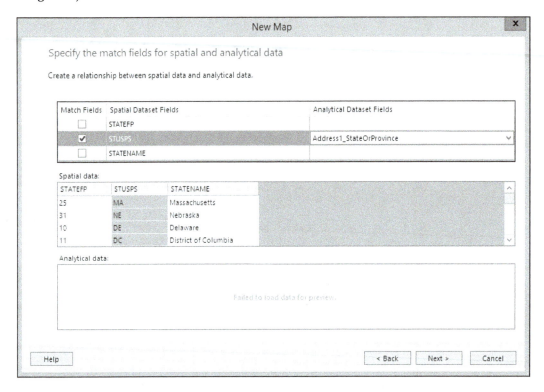

Select the following field options that match the state:

- **STATEFP**: This is an integer value representing the state by a unique identifier
- **STUSPS**: This is the abbreviated state name, such as CA, MA, DE
- **STATENAME**: This states the full state name

We must select at least one matching field to continue; in our case, it is the **STUSPS** field with the **address1_StateOrProvince** field. If we also get the other two matches, it will improve the report's accuracy. Click on the **Next** button to continue.

Dynamics CRM 2011 uses a single line of text for this type of field (state or province). A very common customization among the U.S. customers is to create an option set to show the states with a drop-down combobox.

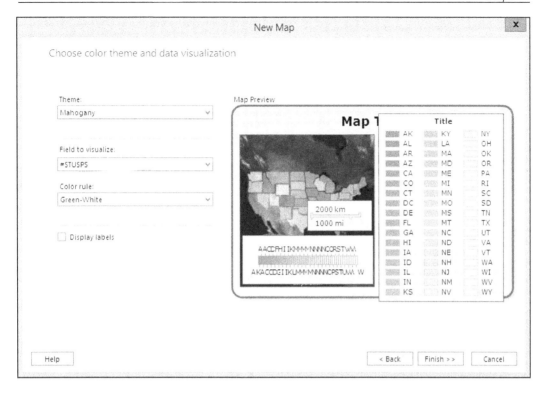

On this screen, we can select the theme (there are six different themes to select from) and if we want the labels to be displayed. We can also select a color rule to configure the color scale we want to use. Click on **Finish** to continue.

Testing the Map report

Click on **Run** to preview the report; it should look similar to the following screenshot.

We should see a darker color on the state; here its value is greater than the value of the lighter colors or when no color is added for the zero value states.

Going back to the design view will allow us to restart the wizard to make changes to the map or add more layers. The layers we can add to the map are:

- Tile layers
- Polygon layers
- Line layers
- Point layers

All these layers can be displayed or hidden based on expressions.

The Report Builder's limitations

Report Builder cannot be used with CRM Online organizations as the Fetch XML data extension is not supported in Report Builder.

Summary

In this chapter, we have created our first report using Report Builder, and we also saw the features we can use that were not available in the standard CRM Report Wizard. We also created an advanced report using the Map Wizard where we can show the records of the U.S. states.

In the next chapter, we are going to learn how to create more complex reports using Visual Studio. Then, we will review the report parameters, charts controls, drill-down and collapsible controls in detail.

5
Creating Contextual Reports

In this chapter we are going to learn how to create more complex reports using Visual Studio, where we are going to cover the following topics:

- Using Visual Studio
- Report parameters in detail
- Charts
- Data sources
- Data sets
- Groups on data sets
- Drill-down and collapsible controls

Using Visual Studio

It is recommended to create a report with the Report Wizard first and then export the **RDL (Report definition language)** file generated by the Report Wizard, and import it on a new Visual Studio Report project. We can also download one of the pre-existing reports that come with the CRM 2011 out of the box (as we saw in *Chapter 3, Creating Your First Report in CRM*, under the *Using Visual Studio* section) and import it on our Visual Studio Report project.

If we take the `Account Distribution` report, for example, and download that report to start a new report, we will see that the report already contains some predefined report parameters. We are going to learn about them in detail in the next section.

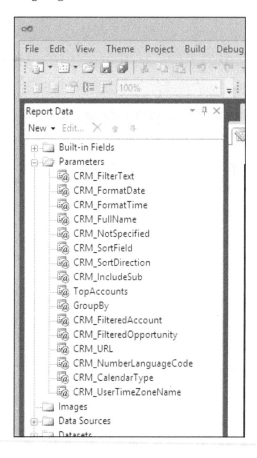

Once we have the report added to our Visual Studio project, we need to change the CRM Data Source connection string so that we can preview the changes before updating the report in CRM.

To do that, expand the **Data Sources** node and double-click on the **CRM** data source, we will see, by default, that the connection string value is set to: **data source=localhost;initial catalog=Adventure_Works_Cycle_MSCRM**

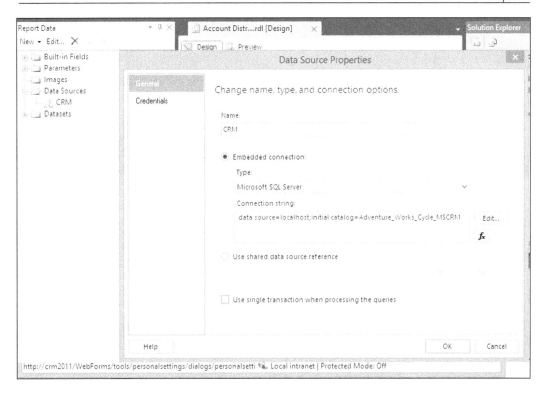

Change local host to our CRM SQL Server name and the **Adventure_Works_Cycle_ MSCRM** value to our CRM organization database. Remember this is usually the name of our organization with the _MSCRM suffix.

Toolbox

In Visual Studio we have the following controls that are inside the toolbox, which we can use on our report:

> If we don't see this toolbox we can go to the **View** menu and then select the **Toolbox** menu option or press *Ctrl + Alt + X*.

- The **Pointer** is not really a control we can add to our report but it is used to be able to select any existing control we have on the report.

- The **Textbox** control is one of the most important controls; it allows us to place text in the report. We can bind the **Textbox** control to any field or expression.

- The **Line** and **Rectangle** controls are graphical controls that allow us to draw lines or rectangles in the report.
- The **Table** and **Matrix** controls are useful for displaying the records of a data set. These two controls also contain **Textbox** inside the column headers and other details as we will see later in this chapter.

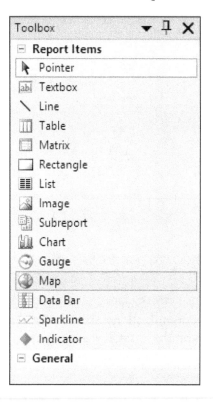

- The **List** control is similar to the **Table** control but with only one column in it.
- The **Subreport** control allows us to include another report, which is also called a subreport, inside the report.
- The **Map** control is used to embed geographic maps in our reports.
- The **Chart**, **Gauge**, **Data Bar**, **Sparkline**, and **Indicator** controls help us in visual representation of the data we want to display.

Expressions

Expression is an advanced way to display data into the report controls. It can contain simple to very complex functions. We can use expressions in any property by taking advantage of the **Expression** editor.

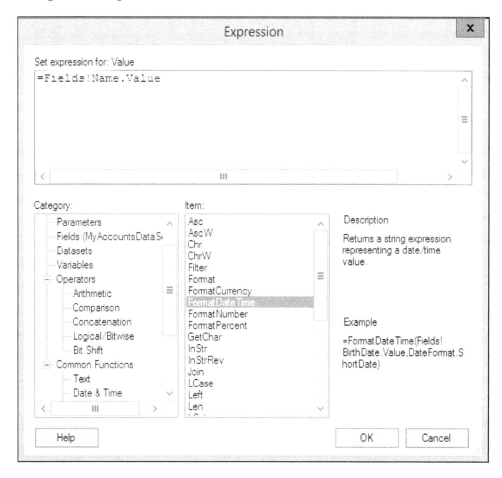

You can refer to the *Appendix, Expression Snippets*, for more details on expressions.

Prefilters

Dynamics CRM has a nice feature named Prefilters. Prefilters allow the user to predefine the records that will be displayed. Regardless of the filters we put on our report queries, we can allow the user to also specify his or her own filter criteria, so that the first time the user opens the report, the following dialog will display:

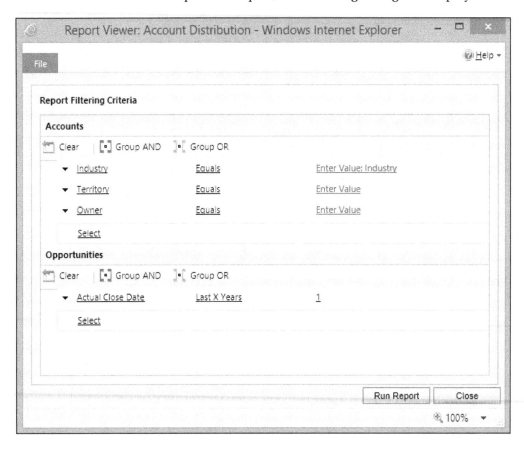

This is an example of how the Account Distribution report uses the prefilters to let the user select what account and opportunities he or she wants to be filtered before running the report. The prefilters need to be properly configured in our report and this can be done in two different ways:

- By using report parameters
- By using the CRMAF_ alias

We will review how to use these two methods in detail in this chapter.

Report parameters in detail

CRM uses some predefined report parameters we can use in our report to get context information about the user and the environment where the report is running. These report parameters are as follows.

CRM_FilterText

`CRM_FilterText` is a hidden parameter that CRM 2011 uses to pass the current prefilters used.

We can display this value on our report by adding a textbox control and assigning it the value `=Parameters!CRM_FilterText.Value`.

As we can see, this is a value that is displayed in the account distribution report under the **Filter Summary** header.

CRM_FormatDate

`CRM_FormatDate` is a parameter that depends on the `DSNumandCurrency` data set that allows us to know what the user date and time configuration are, so we can display the date in the user format he or she has specified on his or her personal settings.

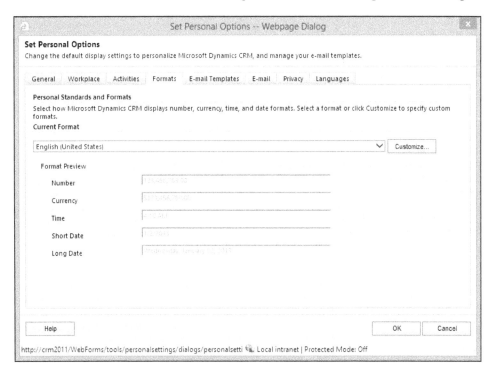

As we can have users located in different countries, some users in the U.S. would like to see the dates in the mm/dd/yyyy format while users in Latin America would like to see dates in the dd/mm/yyyy format.

To display any date field in the user-specific format, we just need to set the format attribute of the textbox control to =Parameters!CRM_FormatDate.Value.

CRM_FormatTime

In a similar way to the CRM_FormatDate parameter, the CRM_FormatTime parameter returns the format of time selected by the user in his or her personal settings.

CRM_FullName

CRM_FullName parameter returns the full name of the user who is running the report, so we can print it on our report by adding a textbox control and setting its value to =Parameters!CRM_FullName.Value.

This is a hidden parameter that depends on the UserInfo data set, which contains the following query:

```
select fullname from FilteredSystemUser where systemuserid = dbo.fn_
FindUserGuid()
```

CRM_FilteredAccount

The parameters containing the filtered view names, such as in this case FilteredAccount, are the prequeries themselves that we can use to pre-filter our queries. This will be used in an SQL query as follows:

```
select * from (' + @CRM_FilteredAccount +') as acct
```

This way only the records pre-filtered by the user running the report will be returned. We can create similar parameters as this for other entities we want to pre-filter in our report, for example, we could create a similar parameter to pre-filter the accounts by creating a parameter with the name of CRM_FilteredAccount and with a default value using a query such as the following:

```
select \[account0\].* from FilteredAccount as "account0"
```

Remember we can also use the CRMAF_ alias in our queries that will provide similar results in the pre-filter lists.

CRM_URL

When running inside Dynamics CRM 2011 application, `CRM_URL` parameter will return the URL of the organization pointing to the `drillopen.aspx` page, for example:

```
http://crmserver/organizationName/CRMReports/viewer/drillopen.aspx
```

This parameter is used when we want to apply drill-down capabilities as we will see in detail later in this chapter.

CRM_CalendarType

`CRM_CalenderType` is a parameter that depends on the `DSNumandCurrency` data set, which allows us to know what the user's calendar configuration is so we can display the dates in the format he or she has specified in his or her personal settings. The `DSNumandCurrency` is a data set that is embedded in all the default predefined reports, so it will be available if we start our report by using any of the currently existing reports.

The query for this database looks as follows:

```
select * from dbo.fn_GetFormatStrings()
```

The different values returned by this parameter can be of the following types:

- **Gregorian**
- **Japanese**
- **Korea**
- **Taiwan**
- **Gregorian US English**
- **Gregorian Arabic**
- **Gregorian Middle East French**
- **Gregorian Transliterated English**
- **Gregorian Transliterated French**

The user can change the calendar by navigating to **File | Options | Formats** and clicking on the **Customize...** button, then going to the **Date** tab. Depending on the language selected, the calendar options will be displayed with a drop-down list; for example, in the Japanese format we can see the following calendar options:

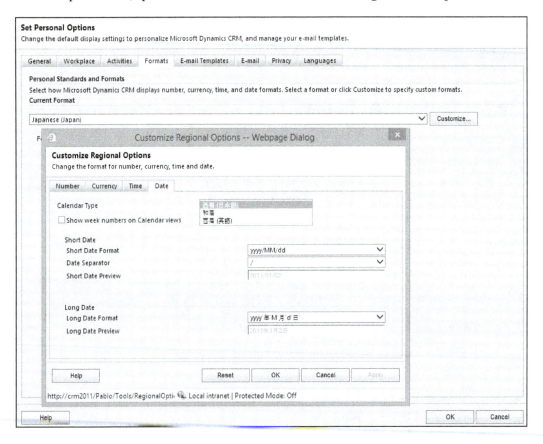

This parameter can then be used within any textbox where we want to display dates by setting the Calendar attribute to this parameter.

 For a complete reference of the CRM parameters, visit `http://msdn.microsoft.com/en-us/library/gg309583.aspx`

Data sources

If we are working with the CRM 2011 on premise version, we can mix data with other data sources in our report; by default, we can create data sources using the following database types:

- Microsoft Dynamics CRM Fetch
- Microsoft SQL Server
- Microsoft SQL Azure
- Microsoft SQL Server Parallel Data Warehouse
- OLE DB
- Microsoft SQL Server Analysis Services
- Oracle
- ODBC
- XML
- Report Server Model
- Microsoft SharePoint List
- SAP Netware BI
- Hyperion Essbase
- TERADATA

For any database type not listed here, we can always find its OLEDB or ODBC adapter to use it in our report.

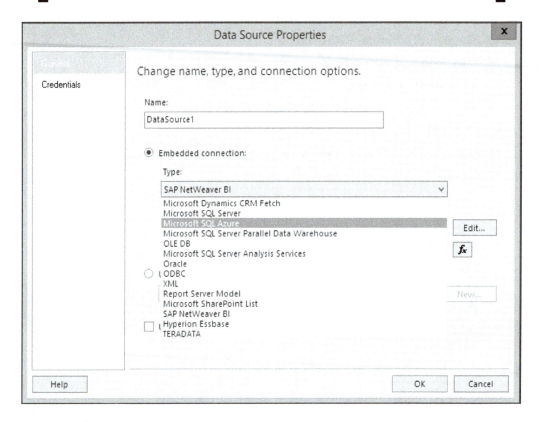

Data sources can be created as either of these two main types:

- Embedded connection
- Using a shared data source reference

Embedded data sources

Embedded data sources means that the data source connection will be embedded within the report (within the RDL file), if we are using this data source for one specific report then this option might be good. However, if we are planning on creating more than one report using the same data source, using the shared data sources will be the best approach.

Shared data sources

Shared data sources are the best option to configure the connection string in one place to update more than one report at the same time; this is the type of data source used by Dynamics CRM. Even though when we work with Visual Studio we see the data source is embedded, it is then changed as soon as we upload the report into Dynamics CRM. This will happen to the CRM data source only, as it is a reserved name for dynamics to use.

The CRM data sources are hidden in the report server, if we open the report manager and go to the organization folder we will see an empty folder.

Clicking on **Details View** will show two hidden data sources; one is used for reports in SQL and the second is used for Fetch XML reports.

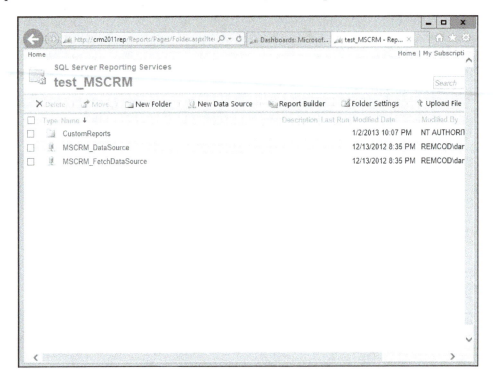

To create a new shared data source to include in our report's project, go to the **Solution Explorer** in Visual Studio and right-click on **Shared Data Sources** and select the **Add new Data Source** menu option.

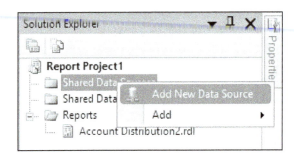

Enter `MyCRMDataSource` in **Name** and select the **Microsoft SQL Server** type, then in **Connection string** enter `data source=crm2011rep;initial catalog=test_MSCRM`

Replace **crm2011rep** with our CRM SQL server name and **test_MSCRM** with our CRM organization database.

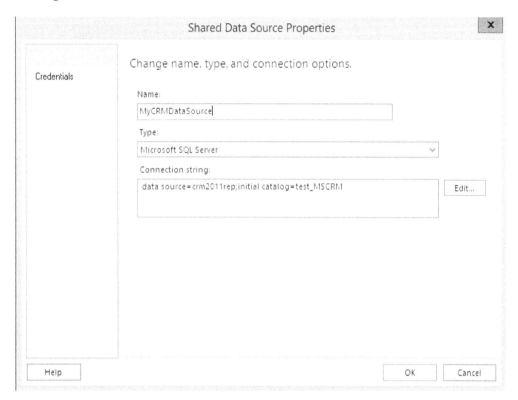

 If we are working on CRM Online organization we won't be able to use the SQL Server type but will have to use the Microsoft Dynamics CRM Fetch type instead.

Click on the **Edit** button to be sure that the authentication is set to **Windows Authentication**, then hit the **Test Connection** button to validate the connection.

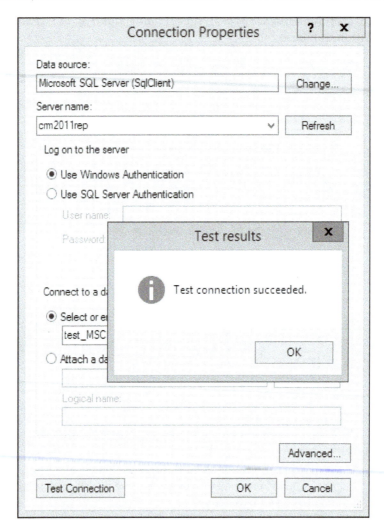

Click on **OK** to close all the open dialog boxes.

Data sets

As with data sources, we can have more than one data set defined in our report; however, each data set is associated with one data source at a time. To create a new Data set follow the given steps:

1. Right-click on the **Datasets** folder and select the **Add Dataset...** menu option:

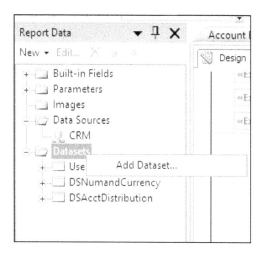

2. When the **Dataset Properties** dialog box opens, we will be presented with the following options:

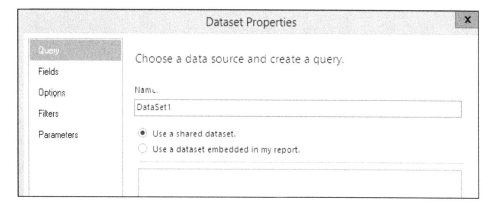

Here we can select to use a shared data set or create a data set that will be embedded in our report; the concept is the same as explained for data sources.

3. If we want to create a shared data set, we will need to cancel this dialog box and go to the **Solution Explorer** window, right-click on the `Shared Datasets` folder, and select the **Add New Dataset** option:

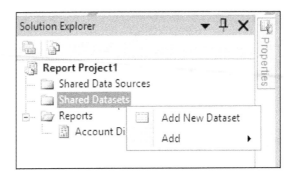

4. When adding a new shared data set we will need to specify the **Data Source**, **Query type**, and **Query**.

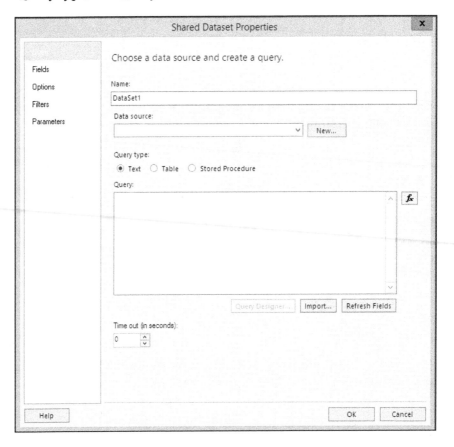

5. Enter `AccountsDataSet` in the **Name** field and select **MyCRMDataSource** from the **Data source** drop-down menu list.

6. We can either write the query manually or use the query designer by clicking on the **Query Designer...** button. When it is open we can add tables by right-clicking on the white textbox and selecting **Add Table...** as shown in the following screenshot:

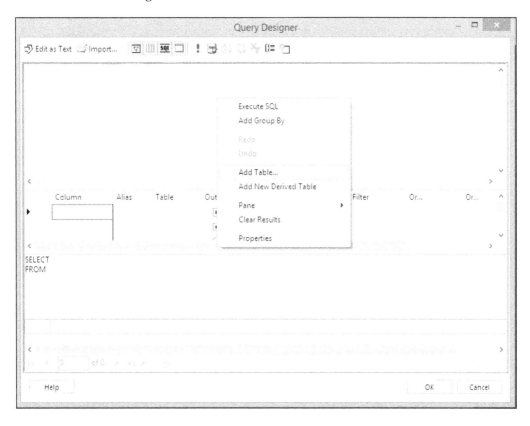

We will be able to either add **Tables**, **Views**, **Functions** or **Synonyms**. We recommend using views as much as possible. If the report is going to be run only by a high-privileged user such as the system administrator, we can use views such as **Account** and **Contact**. However, if our report needs to display results based on the user permissions, we will have to use the Filtered views, where one of these views is present for each entity such as **FilteredAccount** and **FilteredContact**.

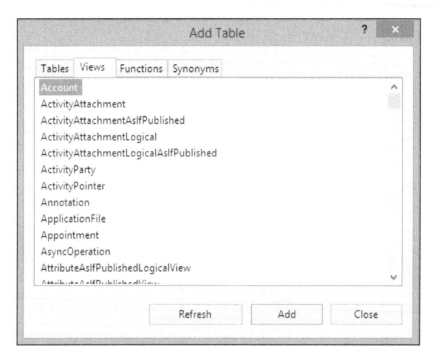

To learn more about the use of Filtered views refer to this link in MSDN http://msdn.microsoft.com/en-us/library/gg328467.aspx. Even though the article says that the only supported way is using Filtered views and the custom SQL-based reports cannot read data directly from the Microsoft Dynamics CRM database tables, I have verified that this is not true and I have to actually avoid them to gain performance for reports that are only intended to be used by system administrators. So I don't need to be worried about the security constraints.

7. Our new data set should look like the following:

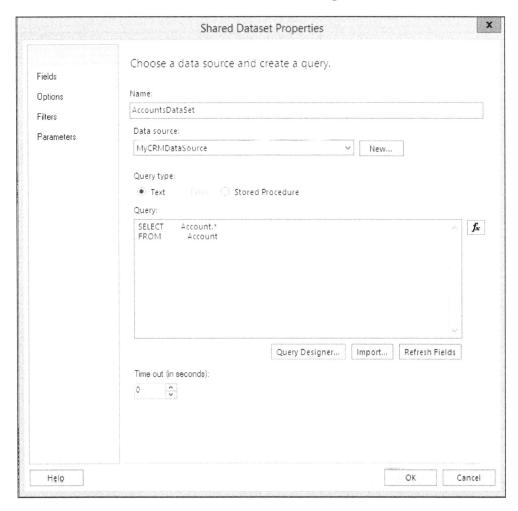

There are some important considerations in this query. In this example, we are using `Select Account.* FROM Account`.

This means that we are not checking the security of the records and might prevent any issue if this report is intended to be used by users that should not be allowed to see some records. If we want to prevent this, we need to change this query to use the Filtered views by using `Select FilteredAccount.* FROM FilteredAccount`.

If we also want to let the user pre-filter the records, we can use the magic of the CRMAF_ alias as follows:

```
Select * FROM FilteredAccount as CRMAF_Account
```

8. The **Fields** tab will allow us to change the field's name or add a custom field to our data set, which can either be **Calculated Field** or **Query Field**.

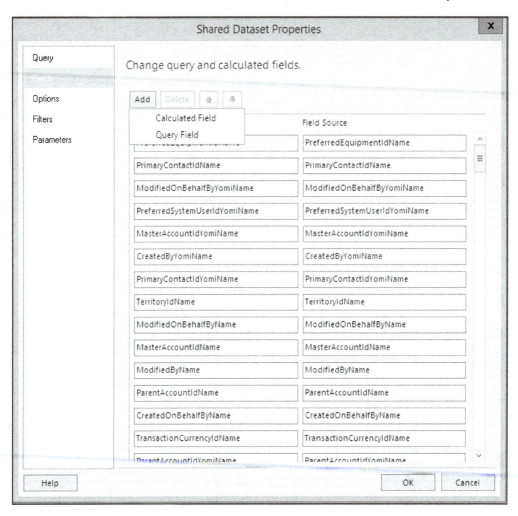

9. The **Options** tab will allow us to configure the **Collation**, **Case sensitivity**, **Accent sensitivity**, **Kanatype sensitivity**, **width sensitivity**, and the **Interpret subtotals as detail rows**. The **Collation**, for example, is important and affects how the data will be sorted; it depends on on the language and country. In most cases we will want to leave the **Default** value for the **Collation** and the **Auto** value for the rest of the options.

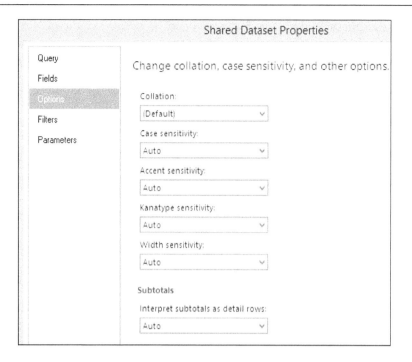

10. The **Filters** tab allows us to add filter criteria to our data set. It is always recommended to apply the filters in the SQL query, but there might be some occasions where we won't be able to, especially when working with a different data source than SQL Server. Here we have a good opportunity to filter the records in our own data set.

11. The **Parameters** tab will allow us to pass the parameters we need, and is used especially , when we are using a stored procedure in our query and need to do some processing before passing the values to it, such as using a function.

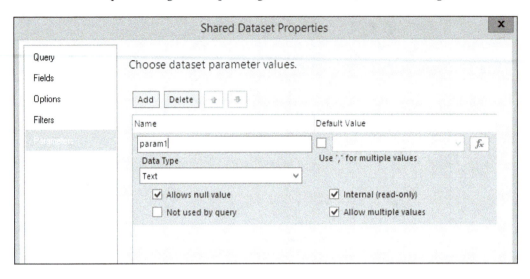

12. Click on **OK** to finish the data set creation. Now, in order to use this new shared data set in our report we will need to go to the **Report Data** window and right-click on the `Datasets` folder and select the **Add Dataset** menu option, where we will be able to use the shared data set we have created earlier.

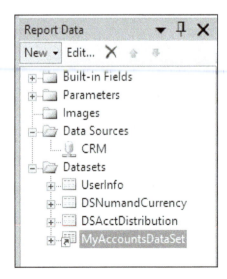

Groups on data sets

To start using a data set we can add a **Table** control to our report and select the data set we created in the **DataSetName** property of the **Table** control as follows:

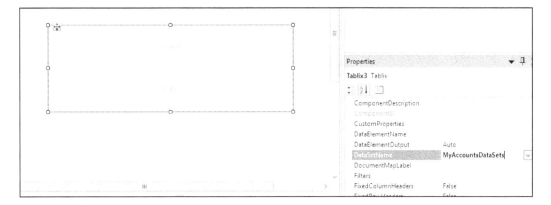

Remember we can usually access the properties window by hitting the *F4* key if it is not visible by default in Visual Studio.

Adding columns to the report

To add a field to the table cells, we move the mouse over the cell we want until we see the blue icon being displayed.

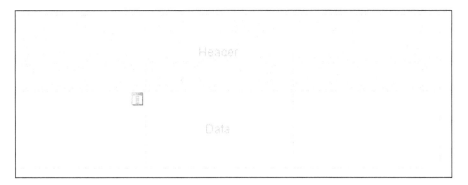

Clicking on the blue icon will display the list of available fields we configure in our data set, so we can easily select the fields we want to display in each cell.

Name	Address1 Country	Address1 Line1
[Name]	[Address1_Country]	[Address1_Line1]

Selecting the fields this way will automatically add the header text with the field name.

To add a new column right-click on the column header and select **Insert Column**, then select **Left** or **Right** depending upon where we want the new column to be located.

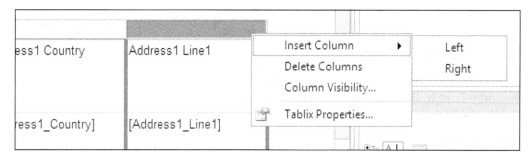

Hiding and showing columns

Selecting the **Column Visibility** will allow us to configure the column visibility based on an expression that can be dynamically updated by, for example, a report parameter using an expression such as =IIf(Parameters!TopAccounts.Value = "1", true, false).

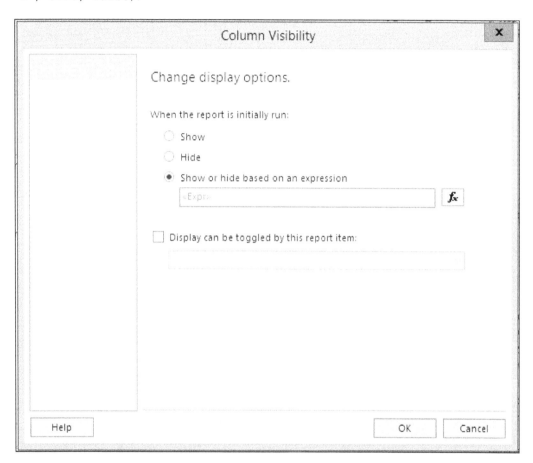

To add another details row to our table we can right-click on the left part of the table and select **Insert Row**:

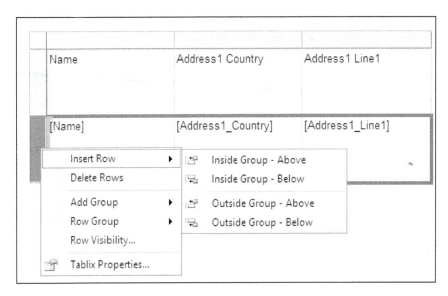

To add a group to our table we can right-click on the left part of the table and select **Add Group**, then select **Parent Group**:

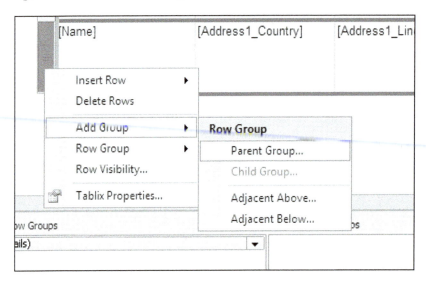

After adding at least one parent group, we can add child groups if we want another level of grouping.

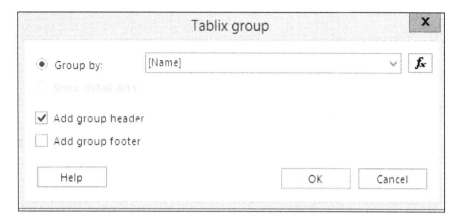

When adding a group we can either specify the field name or use an expression to create a more complex grouping.

Then we can select to add a header and/or a footer for the group in the table. After adding the group we will be able to see it in the table as follows:

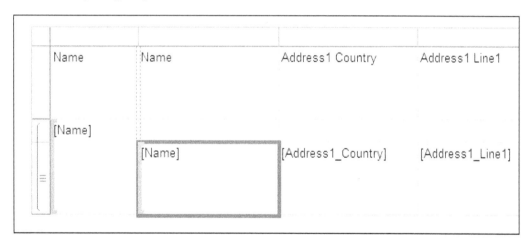

At runtime the report will render showing the groups, as can be seen in the following screenshot:

We can also add **Column Groups** by selecting a field from the **Dataset** window and dragging-and-dropping the field to the **Column Groups** area:

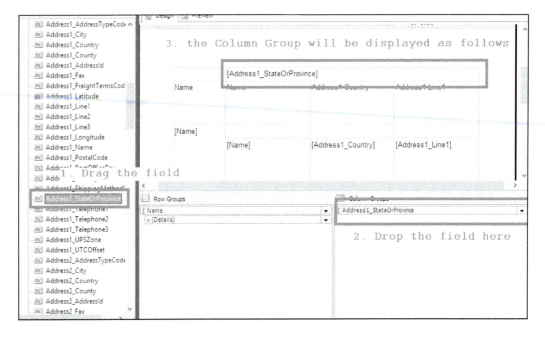

Charts

When working with Visual Studio we can add more powerful charts with more options than the ones presented with the Report Wizard or the Report Builder applications. We are going to create a simple report to show as an example:

1. Drag-and-drop a chart control that is available in the toolbox. We will be presented with a dialog box as shown in the following screenshot:

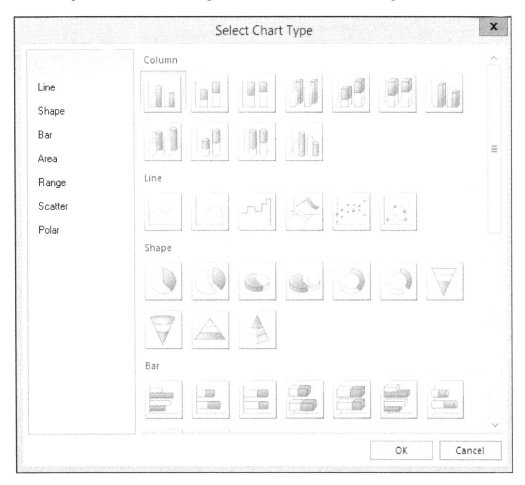

2. For this sample we will select the first chart under the **Column** section and click on **OK**.

3. Click on the columns to configure the fields we want to be displayed. That should open the following properties window to the right of the chart control:

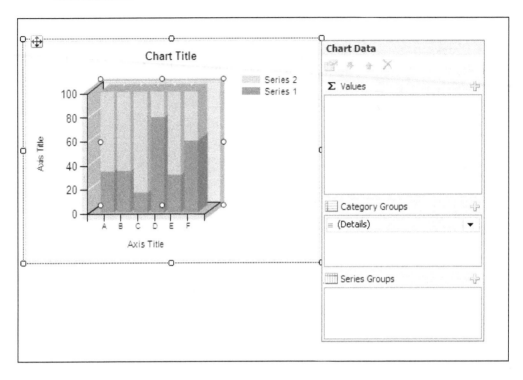

4. Click on the plus sign under the $\sum$ **Values** list, so that we can select the fields that we want to use for aggregation. In this example, we will add **Name** and **EarnedRevenue**. Notice we can also use an expression if we want to create something more complex.

5. We can add different groups of series to display more than one aggregated field by using the **Category Groups** and **Series Groups**.

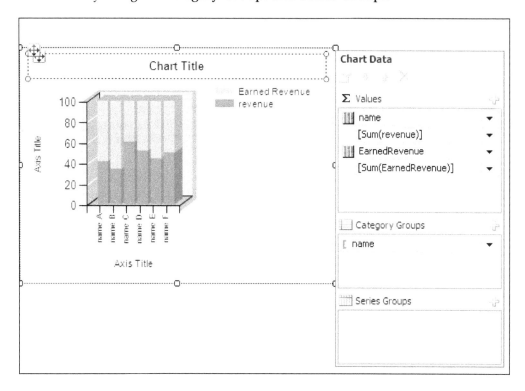

6. Setting the **Category Groups** will configure the field to be used in the Axis.

Drill-down and collapsible controls

If we used groups in our tables, a feature that would be nice to add is the collapsible controls, so that the groups can be collapsed or expanded. To do that we need to select, for example, the controls we want to be hidden or shown, such as the entire row detail, and right-click and select the **Row Visibility...** menu item as follows:

Then check the **Display can be toggled by this report item** checkbox and select the control name, such as the one used on the column header group.

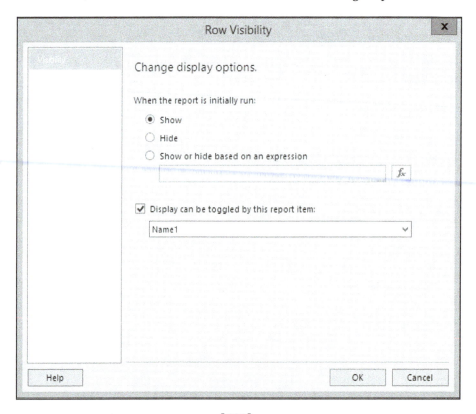

When we run or preview the report we will be able to collapse or expand the rows.

Name	Name	Address1 Country	Address1 Line1
⊟ A. Datum Corporation (sample)			
⊞ Adventure Works (sample)	Adventure Works (sample)	U S	4405 Balboa Court
⊟ Alpine Ski House (sample)			
⊟ Blue Yonder Airlines (sample)			

Summary

In this chapter we looked at the advanced tools and control, we can use to create reports with Visual Studio. We reviewed the CRM Report parameters and the chart controls. We explained the differences between the data source and data sets, and finally we used the groups and drill-down and collapsible controls in our reports.

In the next chapter we are going to see how we can integrate a report with an entity form using web resources.

6
Creating Inline Reports

Inline reports are the ones that are shown inside an entity form. In this chapter we are going to see how we can integrate a report with an entity form using web resources.

Web resources are components we can use to extend the entity form's visualization with custom control capabilities.

Embedding reports on an entity form

In Dynamics CRM 2011 every entity can have more than one form. Each form represents the user interface from where the user can interact with a single-entity record of any entity. There are different types of forms in Dynamics CRM:

- Main
- Mobile

Only the main form type allows the addition of web resources and they are the ones used by the web browser client as well as the outlook client. The mobile form is the one presented to any browser that is not supported by Dynamics CRM, such as those found in a mobile smart phone. By default, only the users with System Administrator and System Customizer roles can customize the entity's forms.

The different controls we can insert into a form are as follows:

- Sections
- Tabs
- Web resources
- Spacer
- Sub-grid
- IFRAME

As we can see, there are no out-of-the-box controls to insert an SQL Reporting Services report into a form, so we will need to create a custom solution to do that, using a web resource.

The web resources we can create in Dynamics CRM 2011 can be any of the following:

- Web Page (HTML)
- Stylesheet (CSS)
- Script (jScript)
- Data (XML)
- Stylesheet (XSL)
- Silverlight (XAP)

We can also store the following image types as web resources:

- PNG format
- JPEG format
- GIF format
- ICO format

Creating a custom solution

The first thing we need to do is create a custom solution; even though this is not required it is recommended so we can easily export the customization to another CRM organization.

1. To create a new solution, go to **Settings** and then click on **Solutions**:

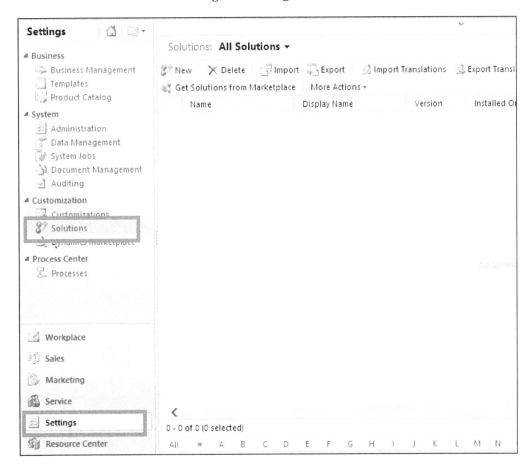

2. Click on **New** to create a new solution. Enter `ReportControl` in the **Display Name** textbox and press the *Tab* key, which will automatically fill the same on the **Name** textbox. Select the default publisher to assign a publisher in the **Publisher** lookup, enter `1` in the **Version** textbox, and then press the *Tab* key. This will automatically add `.0.0.0` to the version text. Your solution screen should look like the following:

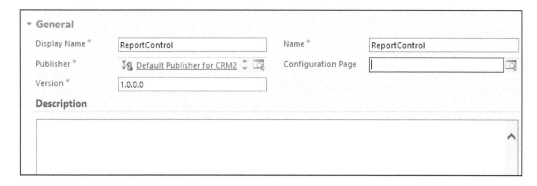

3. Click on the **Save** icon to save the solution that will enable the sitemap links.

Creating the HTML web resource

The next thing we need to do is to create a web resource of the HTML type. This type of web resource will allow us to embed HTML code inside the entity form.

1. Click on **Web Resources** and then on **New**:

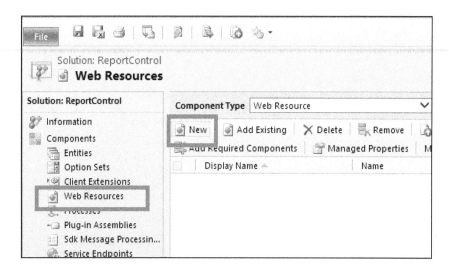

2. Enter reportcontrol in the **Name** field, then enter Report Control on the **Display Name** textbox, and select the **Web Page (HTML)** option under the **Type** option set. Your web resource should look like the following:

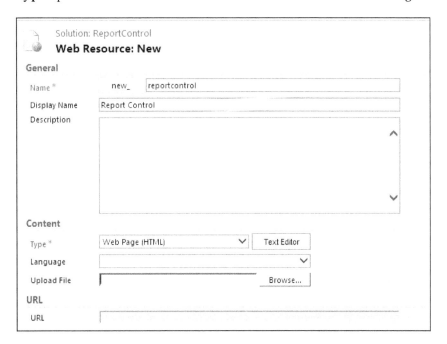

3. Click on the **Text Editor** button, then click on the **Source** tab and remove the code that appears by default, and write the code that is available for download on http://www.packtpub.com/support.

```
<HTML><HEAD>
<SCRIPT src="ClientGlobalContext.js.aspx"></SCRIPT>
<SCRIPT language=javascript>
      function SetReport() {
          var Parameters =
          qs("data").toString().split('%2a');
          var id = Parameters[0];

          if (!IsGuid(id)) {
              var msg = "Please enter a valid report ID
              in the Custom Parameter (data) box.";
              msg += "\n\nMake sure that %7b from the
              beginning and %7d from the end of the link
              are not included in the report ID."
              alert(msg);
              return;
          }
```

```
var serverAndOrgUrl =
document.location.toString().split('%')[0];
var iframeSrc = null;
    iframeSrc = serverAndOrgUrl +
    'crmreports/viewer/viewer.aspx?action=
    run&id=%7b' + id + '%7d';


var report = document.createElement("iframe");
report.setAttribute('id', 'reportFrame');
report.setAttribute('name', 'reportFrame');
report.setAttribute('src', iframeSrc);
report.setAttribute('height', '100%');
report.setAttribute('width', '100%');
report.setAttribute('scrolling', 'auto');
report.setAttribute('frameborder', '0');
report.onreadystatechange = ShowFrame;

var reportDiv = document.createElement("div");
reportDiv.setAttribute('height', '100%');
reportDiv.setAttribute('width', '100%');
reportDiv.appendChild(report);
document.body.appendChild(reportDiv);

function ShowFrame() {
    if (report.readyState == "complete") {
        menubar = report.contentWindow.
        document.getElementById('mnuBar1');
        if (menubar != null) {
            menubar.style.display = "none";
        }


        editFilter = report.contentWindow.
        document.getElementById
        ('trEditFilter');
        if (editFilter != null) {
            editFilter.style.display = "none";
        }
    }
}
function PassIdValues() {
    var WebResource = document.getElementById
    ('reportViewer_ctl04_ctl04_txtValue');
```

```
                    var ListIdTextBox = document.getElementById
                    ('reportViewer_ctl04_ctl04_txtValue');

            }

            function qs(search_for) {
            // this function is used to parse the query
            string parameters
                    var query = window.location.
                    search.substring(1);
                    var parms = query.split('&');
                    for (var i = 0; i < parms.length; i++) {
                        var pos = parms[i].indexOf('=');
                        if (pos > 0 && search_for ==
                        parms[i].substring(0, pos)) {
                            return parms[i].substring(pos + 1);
                        }
                    }
                    return "";
            }

            function getServerUrl() {
            // this function is used to get the CRM Server
            URL
                    context = GetGlobalContext();
                    return context.getServerUrl();
            }

            function IsGuid(guid) {
            // Validates if the parameter is a valid GUID
                    if (guid != null) {
                        var guidRegEx = /^([0-9a-fA-F]){8}-
                        ([0-9a-fA-F]){4}-([0-9a-fA-F]){4}-
                        ([0-9a-fA-F]){4}-([0-9a-fA-F]){12}$/;
                        return guidRegEx.test(guid);
                    }
                    return false;
            }
        }
    }
</SCRIPT>

<META charset="utf-8"></HEAD>
<BODY onload="SetReport()" style="MARGIN: 0px"></BODY></HTML>
```

4. Your web resource should look like the following:

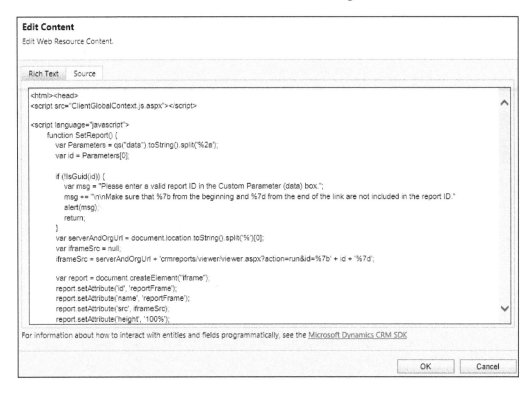

5. Click on the **OK** button to close this dialog. Now click on **Save** and then on **Publish**.

Let's look a little more at the code we wrote above and what it does. As we can see, in the last line of the code, the web resource does not have a lot of HTML code but instead it calls the SetReport function in the BODY.onload event attribute.

The SetReport function initially parses the web resource parameters to obtain the report ID, as we will see in the next section of this chapter when implementing the report control.

If the report parameter is not a valid GUID, an error will be displayed to the user. Then it prepares the IFRAME URL for the report using the GUID of the report.

Next an IFRAME element is created dynamically so it can host the report viewer URL. After the IFRAME is loaded, there is a function defined with the name of `ShowFrame` that checks when the report is loaded so it can hide the menu toolbar added by the CRM report viewer page.

The reference to the JavaScript file `ClientGlobalContext.js.aspx` added to the top of the code is necessary to be able to use the method `context.getServerUrl()` to know the CRM server URL. This is based on the context of where it is running as it might be different, depending on whether we are running on an on-premises environment, CRM online, or an IFD environment.

 There is also a CodePlex managed solution you can download from `http://reportingondashboard.codeplex.com/`, which is very similar to the solution proposed here.

Implementing the report control

Now that we have the control ready, we can now use it on any entity form. We are going to see an example here of how to use it on the out-of-the-box Account Overview report in the account form.

1. Go to **Accounts** and click on **New** to open the account form. Then move to the **Customize** tab and click on the **Form** button on the ribbon under the **Design** group:

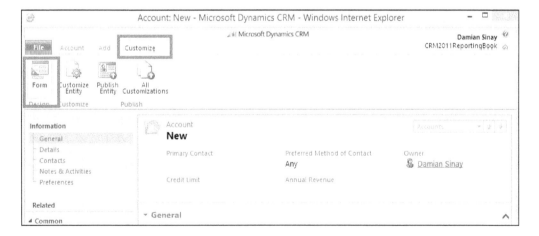

2. This will open the **Account** form in design mode. Click on the section where you want the `Report Control` page to be placed and move to the **Insert** tab. In this example we select the **General** section.

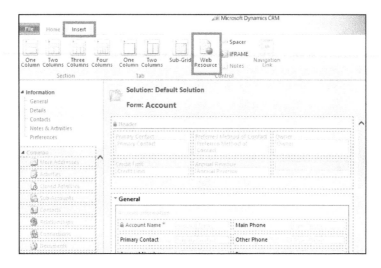

3. Click on the **Web Resource** icon and locate the web resource to assign it to the **Web Resource** lookup. Enter a name in the **Name** textbox such as `ReportControl`. Pressing the *Tab* key will autopopulate the **Label** textbox.

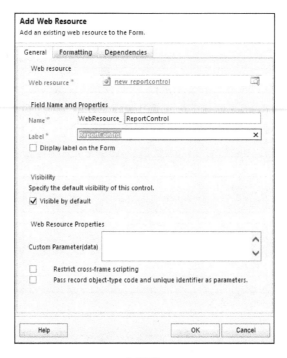

4. To display the **Account Overview** report, we need to specify the GUID of the report as a custom parameter to the control. To get the GUID of the report, go to **Reports** and right-click on the **Account Overview** report. Then select the **Copy a Link** menu option as shown:

5. This will copy the following onto the clipboard:

   ```
   http://crm2011/CRM2011ReportingBook/crmreports/viewer/viewer.
   aspx?id=%7b232668A8-7960-E211-8E84-00155DFE7909%7d
   ```

   After the question mark symbol you will see the ID parameter, from where you need to remove the %7b from the beginning of the value and also remove the %7d from the end of the text. So your report ID will be 232668A8-7960-E211-8E84-00155DFE7909.

6. Copy this ID and go back to the web resource properties page and paste it to the **Custom Parameter(data)** textbox as follows:

7. It is a good practice to extend the height of the control, as by default it will only use six rows. In order to do that, click on the **Formatting** tab and change the **Number of Rows** value from 6 to 10 and optionally select the **Automatically expand to use available space** checkbox.

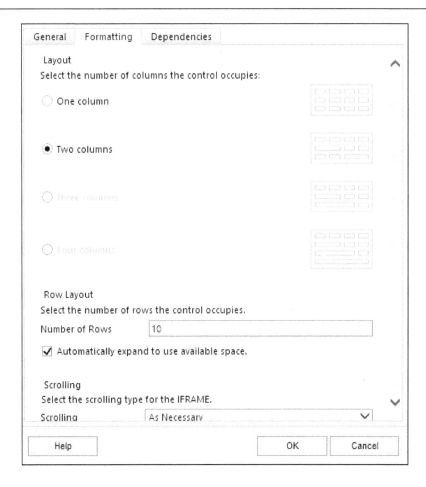

8. Click on **OK** to save the changes. Then go back to the **Home** tab and click on the **Save** button on the form and select **Publish**:

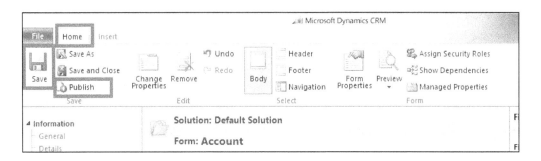

Close the form designer window and close the new account form you opened before.

9. To test the solution go to the **Account** tab and open any account record. You will see the report displayed inside the form as follows:

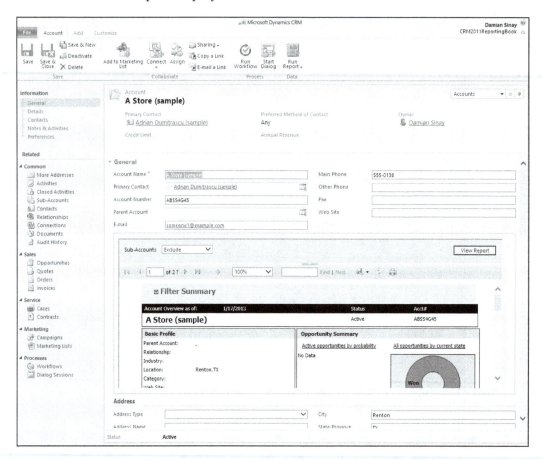

Developer Toolkit

If we want to have this solution packaged in a way that we can use Visual Studio to edit the HTML web resources, we can use the Developer Toolkit that comes with the Microsoft Dynamics CRM SDK. The SDK can be downloaded from http://www.microsoft.com/en-us/download/details.aspx?id=24004.

1. Inside the `sdk\tools\developertoolkit` folder there are two installers. The `crmdevelopertools_installer.msi` installer is the one used for Visual Studio 2010 while the `crmdevelopertoolsvs12_installer.msi` installer is used for Visual Studio 2012.

2. After installing this toolkit you will be able to create a Dynamics CRM 2011 project template that will connect to Dynamics CRM 2011. When creating a new project, you can select the **Dynamics CRM Package** project template as shown in the following screenshot:

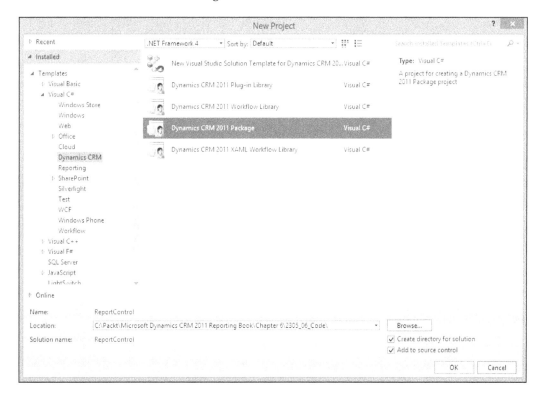

If you don't see the templates, be sure the target framework is selected as **.NET Framework 4**.

3. Enter a name for your project, say `ReportControl`, and click on **OK**. You will be asked to connect to a Dynamics CRM 2011 server. Enter the name and the port number of the CRM server you want to connect to. The default protocol selected is **HTTPS**. For this, the port number to be entered is `443`. Whereas, if you have **HTTP** selected, the default port number to use will be `80`. If you are working with the CRM Online version, you will need to enter `disco.crm.dynamics.com` in the CRM **Discovery Server Name** textbox.

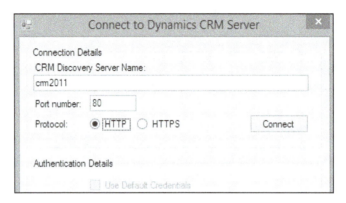

4. Click on **Connect** if you are working with CRM on premise. You can check the **Use Default Credentials** checkbox. If you are working with CRM Online you will need to provide the **User name** and **Password** only.

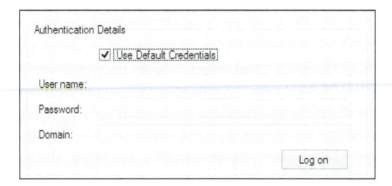

5. Click on the **Log on** button and you will be able to select the organization. All organizations you have permissions to access will be displayed in the **Organization** drop-down list.

6. After selecting the organization you will be able to select a solution from the **Solution Name** drop-down list. Select the solution you want to bind to the Visual Studio project.

Click on **OK** to connect and close this dialog.

7. When the project is created you will see the following project structure in the **Solution Explorer** window:

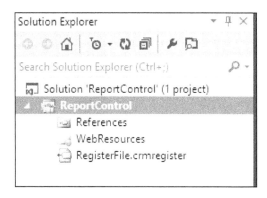

8. As you can see, the `WebResources` folder is empty, so we will need to add the web resource we already created before. To do that, you will need to go to the **CRM Explorer** window, which you can open by going to the **View** menu and selecting the **CRM Explorer** menu option as follows:

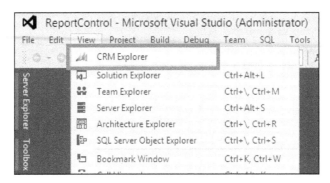

9. This will open the following window from where you will be able to locate the web resource by expanding the organization name node, which is **CRM2011ReportingBook** in our case. Then, by expanding the **Web Resources** node and the **Web Page (HTML)** you should be able to see the `Report Control` HTML page we created. Right-click on this file and select **Add to packaging project**:

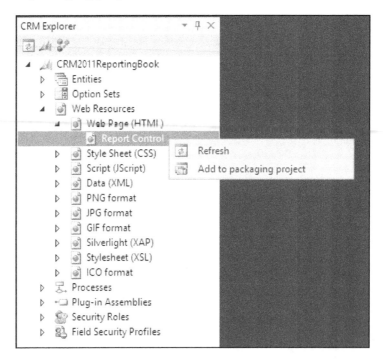

10. Doing this will add the web resource to our project. This will enable us to see it in the **Solution Explorer** window (see the following screenshot showing the **Solution Explorer** window), allowing us to make it part of a Team Foundation server project so that we can have source control and a history of the changes made.

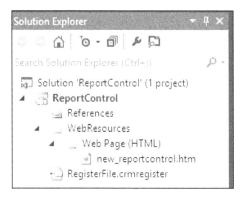

11. There is another benefit of using the Developer Toolkit, which is the ability to edit the HTML web resources with a powerful editor where the text is displayed in color. And having IntelliSense is also a great benefit (see the following screenshot with the code editor).

```
new_reportcontrol.htm

1   <HTML><HEAD>
2   <SCRIPT src="ClientGlobalContext.js.aspx"></SCRIPT>
3
4   <SCRIPT language=javascript>
5        function SetReport() {
6            var Parameters = qs("data").toString().split('%2a');
7            var id = Parameters[0];
8            var listId = document.parentWindow.parent.document.location.toString
9            if (!IsGuid(id)) {
10               var msg = "Please enter a valid report ID in the Custom Paramete
11               msg += "\n\nMake sure that %7b from the beginning and %7d from
12               alert(msg);
13               return;
14           }
15           var serverAndOrgUrl = document.location.toString().split('%')[0];
16           var iframeSrc = null;
17           if (Parameters.length > 1) {
18               iframeSrc = serverAndOrgUrl + 'crmreports/viewer/viewer.aspx?ac
19           }
20           else {
21               iframeSrc = serverAndOrgUrl + 'crmreports/viewer/viewer.aspx?ac
22           }
23
24           var report = document.createElement("iframe");
25           report.setAttribute('id', 'reportFrame');
26           report.setAttribute('name', 'reportFrame');
```

12. Using the Developer Toolkit allows us to easily deploy any change we make on the HTML web resources by right-clicking on the solution name and selecting the **Deploy Solution** option:

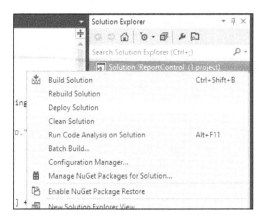

13. Notice that after deploying the solution it is likely that we will need to publish the changes we made to the web resources we updated. In order to do that we need to go to the **CRM Explorer** and double-click on the web resource we want to publish. This will open the web resource properties page inside Visual Studio so we can click on the **Publish** button.

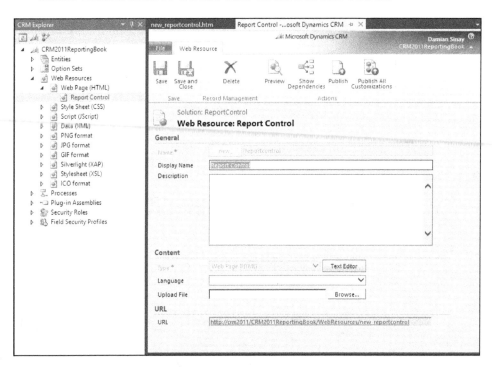

14. The Developer Toolkit has some nice shortcuts. To open the CRM organization web client, click on the second icon at the top of the **CRM Explorer** window. Clicking on the third icon will open the **Solution** window.

15. The project properties windows, which you can open by right-clicking on the project name in the **Solution Explorer** window and selecting the properties window, present the option to export the solution file on every deployment if you set it to True under the **Deploy** tab.

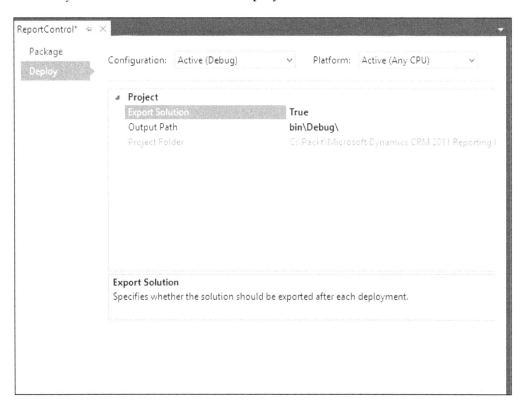

16. It is very important that you set up a name for the **Output name** textbox (see the following screenshot) in the **Package** tab, or your solution zip file won't be created and no error will be displayed.

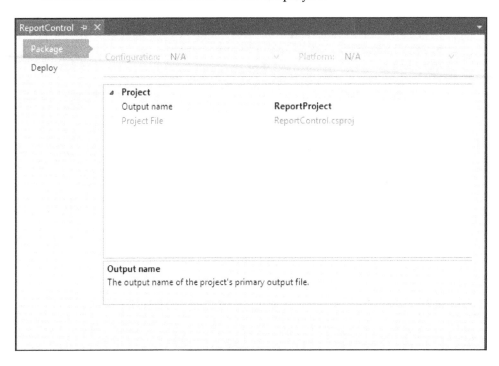

17. The solution generated will be in unmanaged state, so it won't be good for distribution, but will be good to have a deployment backup if you want to move the solution to another development organization.

A very important consideration while having a CRM project integrated with a source control is to be sure that you have the RegisterFile.crmregister file checked out when doing deployments, as these files get updated on every deployment and, if you don't have it checked out, you will receive an error.

The error message you will get will be as follows:

```
Error4Error registering plugins and/or workflows.
The resource string "ErrorSerializingRegFile" for the "RegisterPlugin"
task cannot be found.
Confirm that the resource name "ErrorSerializingRegFile" is correctly
spelled, and the resource exists in the task's assembly.  C:\Program
Files (x86)\MSBuild\Microsoft\CRM\Microsoft.CrmDeveloperTools.12.
targets
176    4ReportControl
```

As you can see, the error message does not relate to the real cause of the problem, which is related to the `RegisterFile.crmregister` file. This file needs to be writable (not read-only) as the source control sets the files to read-only when they are checked in. Checking out this file will solve this problem.

Summary

In this chapter, we looked at how we can embed a report inside any entity form by creating a custom solution that uses an HTML web resource. We have also seen how to implement this custom solution on the account entity using the account overview report. We then reviewed the Developer Toolkit, which helps us to work in a more organized manner with custom CRM solutions, getting the benefit of IntelliSense and a deployment capability, which also allows us to integrate our source code with a source controller software such as Team Foundation Server.

In the next chapter we are going to see how we can integrate a report in a dashboard and review the basic and advanced features of the chart controls that come with Dynamics CRM 2011.

7
Using Reports and Charts in Dashboard

In this chapter we are going to see how we can integrate a report in a dashboard and we are going to review the basic and advanced features of the chart controls that come with Dynamics CRM 2011.

Showing report on a dashboard

We can use the same solution that we built in the last chapter to display a report on a dashboard. Microsoft Dynamics CRM 2011 introduces a new feature called Dashboard from where we can mix different types of representation of our data on a simple page. The dashboards are located by default in the **Workplace** area under **My Work**.

There are two types of dashboards:

- Personal dashboards
- System dashboards

The personal dashboards are the ones that we can create from this interface when clicking on the **New** button that is located in the ribbon. We can also share it with other users by using the **Share Dashboard** button:

The system dashboards are the ones that are created when we go to **Settings | Customizations | Customize the system** this way we will create dashboards in the Default Solution; we can also create a custom solution and add them there.

System dashboards are visible to all users. The components that we can add to a dashboard are as follows:

- Chart
- List
- Web Resource
- Iframe

To create a new dashboard, click on **New**.

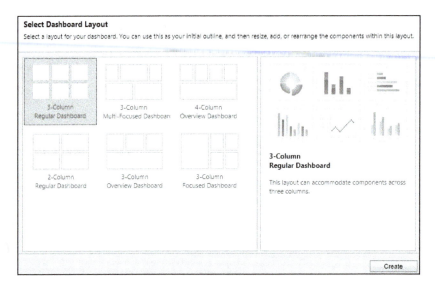

Select the layout you want (in this case we will select the first layout) and click on **Create**.

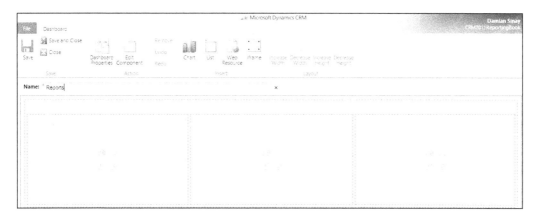

Click on **Web Resource** to locate the report control web resource that we have created. It is similar to what we did when including the web resource on the entity form (as we saw in the previous chapter). We need to pass the report ID that we want to display on the dashboard. We do this in the **Custom Parameter (data)** textbox.

Click on **OK** to insert the web resource on our dashboard. To make it look better, click three times on the **Increase Width** button on the ribbon so it will fit the entire width of the dashboard, then click on the **Increase Height** button five times.

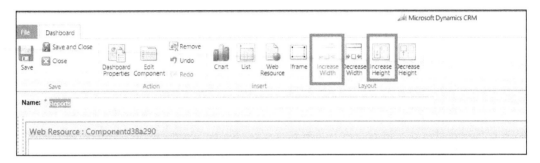

Note that even though the default template comes with only two rows, we can add more rows if we want by clicking on the main area of the dashboard (not inside any cell). Inserting any component will automatically add it on a new row. However, there are a maximum of six rows allowed per dashboard.

Enter a name for the dashboard and click on the **Save and Close** button from the ribbon. We will see our report inside the dashboard as follows:

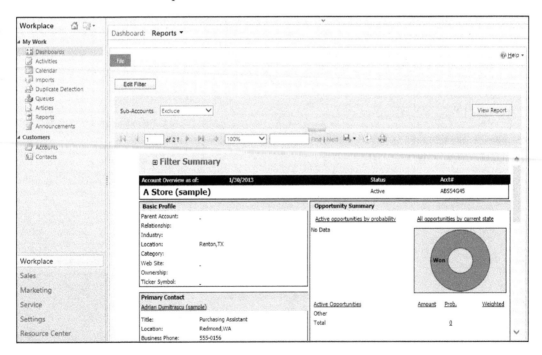

To learn more about dashboards I recommend the book *Microsoft Dynamics CRM 2011: Dashboards Cookbook, MVP Mark AuCoin, Packt Publishing* (`http://www.packtpub.com/microsoft-dynamics-crm-2011-for-creating-customizing-interacting-dashboards-Cookbook/book`).

Exporting dashboards

To copy a system dashboard to another CRM organization, we will need to create a solution and include the dashboard that we created if we used the default solution.

 We cannot export and copy personal dashboards to other Dynamics CRM organizations.

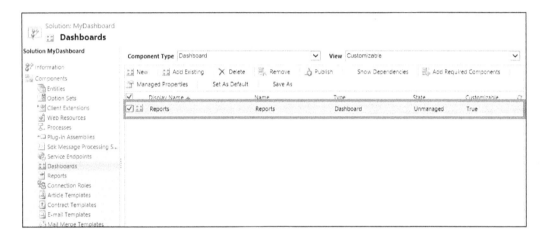

When we export a solution that contains a dashboard and expand the solution zip file, we will see the dashboard XML representation in the `customization.xml` file as follows:

```
<Dashboards>
  <Dashboard>
    <LocalizedNames>
      <LocalizedName description="Reports" languagecode="1033" />
    </LocalizedNames>
    <FormId>{54ebdaa6-be6e-e211-b407-00155dfe7909}</FormId>
    <IsCustomizable>1</IsCustomizable>
    <IsDefault>0</IsDefault>
    <FormXml>
```

```xml
<forms type="dashboard">
  <form>
    <tabs>
      <tab showlabel="false" verticallayout="true"
id="{6669382b-2a96-4dae-b350-063a30f14187}">
        <labels>
          <label description="Tab" languagecode="1033" />
        </labels>
        <columns>
          <column width="100%">
            <sections>
              <section showlabel="false" showbar="false"
columns="1111" id="{01451b67-28f2-471e-9a94-794bd73e91f6}">
                <labels>
                  <label description="Section"
languagecode="1033" />
                </labels>
                <rows>
                  <row>
                    <cell colspan="4" rowspan="18"
showlabel="false" id="{d42521be-0876-43b0-958a-eb4c46ccbf54}">
                      <labels>
                        <label description="Componentdb2e481"
languagecode="1033" />
                      </labels>
                      <control id="WebResource_
Componentdb2e481" classid="{9FDF5F91-88B1-47f4-AD53-C11EFC01A01D}">
                        <parameters>
                          <Url>new_reportcontrol</Url>
                          <ShowInROF>false</ShowInROF>
                          <PassParameters>false</
PassParameters>
                          <Security>false</Security>
                          <Scrolling>auto</Scrolling>
                          <Border>true</Border>
                        </parameters>
                      </control>
                    </cell>
                  </row>
                </rows>
```

```
            </section>
          </sections>
        </column>
      </columns>
    </tab>
  </tabs>
</form>
</forms>
</FormXml>
</Dashboard>
</Dashboards>
```

 To understand more about the dashboard XML format go to http://msdn.microsoft.com/en-us/library/gg334200.aspx.

Basic charts

Dynamics CRM 2011 introduces a new feature called Charts that helps us add charts easily without the need to create a report for that purpose. To create a chart we can either create a solution, which is always the recommended method, or go to **Settings | Customizations | Customize the System**. It will be using the Default Solution.

As with dashboards we can have two types of charts:

- Personal charts
- System charts

Personal charts are the ones that we can create from the entity we want. They can be created by going to the **Charts** tab on the ribbon and clicking on the **New Chart** button. These charts will be only be visible to us and they can be shared with other users.

System charts can be created from a Solution or by going to **Settings | Customizations | Customize the System**. It will be using the Default Solution. These charts will be visible to all users.

Charts depend on the entity, so we will look at them under each entity; for example, the account entity comes with the following out-of-the-box predefined charts:

- **Accounts by Industry**
- **Accounts by Owner**
- **Accounts by Territories**
- **New Accounts by Month**

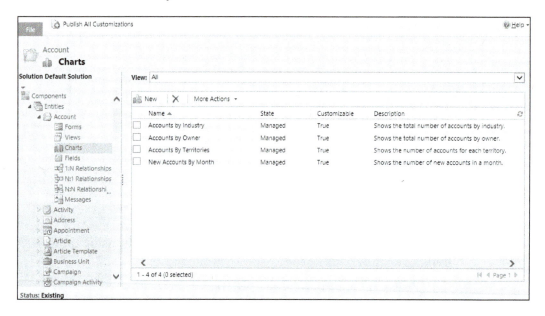

To create a new chart, click on **New**. This will display the chart editor, which we will see in detail later in this chapter.

The differences between charts and a report to display graphical representation of the data is that charts don't have the ability to easily print or export the chart to different formats like the reports can.

Each chart depends on a View and this is because they are somehow related, meaning that the charts can be displayed along with the views as well. So for example in the account entity, depending on what view we are in, we will have the ability to display the charts associated to that view.

If we click on the right part of the screen where it says **Click here to view the Chart**, the charts will be displayed as follows:

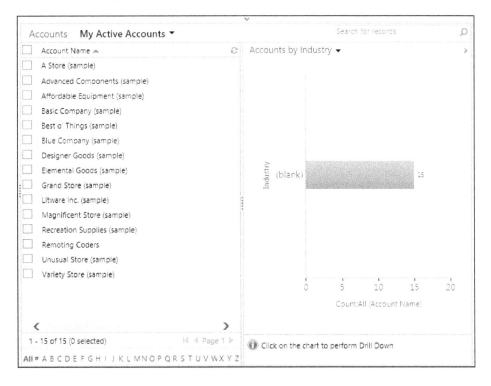

Clicking on the chart name will allow us to change the chart:

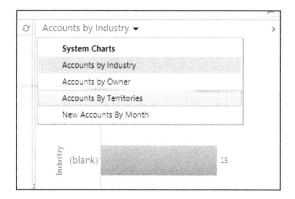

Drill-down chart

Charts also have a very nice feature called drill down, which allows us to get more detailed results based on a selected field. If we click on the bar for which we want detailed results, we will be presented with a dialog that will allow us to select the field that we want the chart to be filtered on. For example, if we are looking at the **Accounts by Industry** chart in the account entity, we can click on the bar and we will see the available options.

These options allow us to select a field as well as to change the type of chart that we want to be displayed for that field.

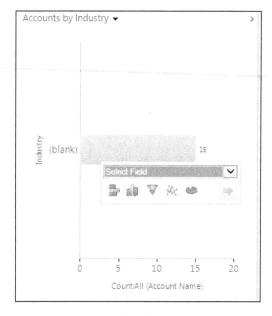

If we select a field and any of the chart types and then click on the arrow, we will see a new chart grouped by the new field we selected:

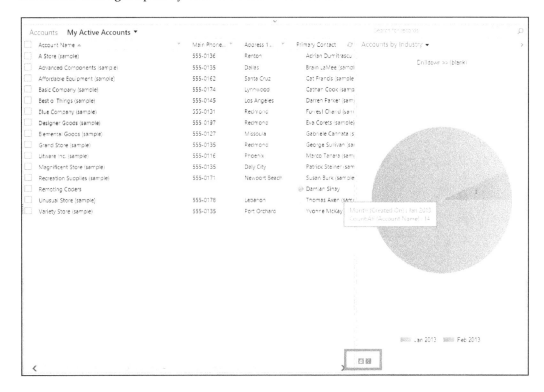

When we entered into the drill-down mode a new set of buttons will appear on the bottom part. The first button that shows a home on the icon allows us to return to the first view of the chart while the second icon is a right arrow that allows us to go back to the previous drill-down filter as we can drill-down on a chart several times.

Notice that using the drill down affects the records displayed by the view. Hovering the mouse over the chart shows us a legend with more details of the portion of the chart we are looking for.

We can change the position of the chart and views if we don't want the chart to be displayed on the right-hand side of the screen by going to the top ribbon and clicking on the **Charts** tab. There is a button called **Chart Pane** that has the following options:

- **Right**
- **Top**
- **Off**

Notice that clicking on the **New** button will also allow us to create a new chart. If you select the **Top** option it will show the chart on top and the grid view on the bottom, as shown in the following screenshot:

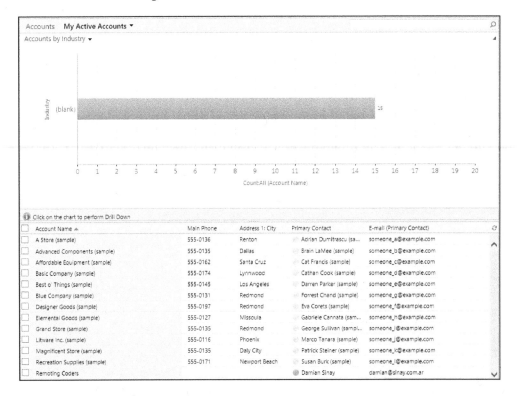

Charts editor

The chart editor has a ribbon from where we can select the type of chart we want to use. We can select one of the following options:

- **Column**
- **Bar**
- **Area**
- **Line**
- **Pie**
- **Funnel**

The **Column** type chart has the following subtypes:

- **Column**
- **Stacked Column**
- **100% Stacked Column**

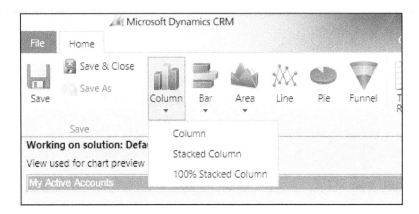

The **Bar** type chart has the following subtypes:

- **Bar**
- **Stacked Bar**
- **100% Stacked Bar**

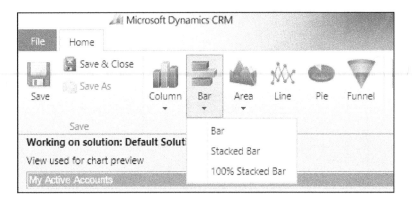

The **Area** type chart has the following subtypes:

- **Area**
- **Stacked Area**
- **100% Stacked Area**

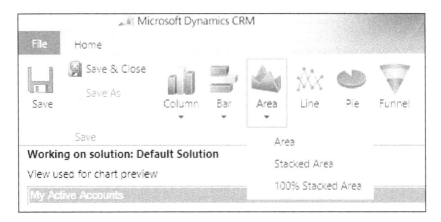

Once we select the type of chart we want, we need to select the fields that we want to display in the legends as well as the fields that we want to be used in the categories. Entering the name is not required as it will be formed right after we select the fields.

For each **Legend Entries (Series)** field, we can select from one of the following aggregated functions:

- **Avg**
- **Count:All**
- **Count non empty**
- **Max**
- **Min**
- **Sum**

For example, if we select **Account Name** in the **Legend Entries** field and **Address1: County** in the **Horizontal (Category) Axis Labels** field, it will automatically fill in the name **Account Name by Address 1: County** as shown in the following screenshot:

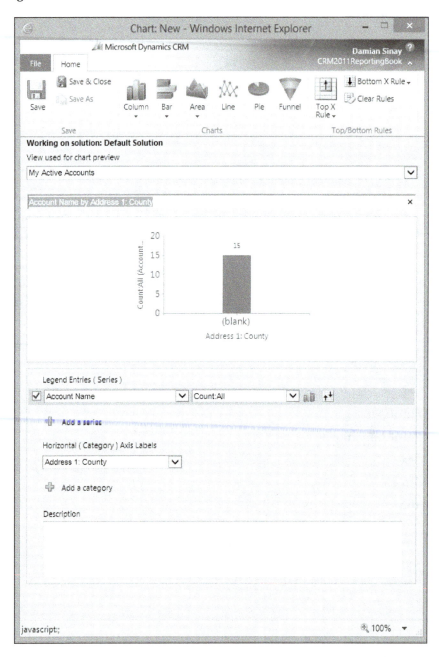

We will also see a preview of the chart right after we select the fields so we can play with the different fields until we get the desired look and feel for the chart. For example, there might be cases where the records are too much to be displayed nicely on a chart; in that case we will need to minimize the number of bars displayed by using the Top X Rules.

For example, if we select **Address1: Line 1** as the **Horizontal (Category) Axis Labels** field, we will see the chart with lots of bars. Having lots of bars on a chart makes it very difficult to understand.

This will be a good example where we would like to display just the top five items by using the **Top X Rule** and selecting **Top 5 Items** as follows:

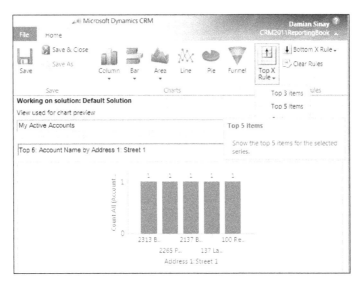

To remove the rules selected, we can click on the **Clear Rules** button. Using the **Bottom X Rule** will have the reverse effect of the **Top X Rule** where only the bottom five items will be displayed.

We can either add more series or categories to the chart but not both at the same time. Finally, we can optionally add a description to the chart in the **Description** box.

Exporting charts

In order to copy the System charts we created to another organization, we will need to create a new solution and include the entity from where we created the chart.

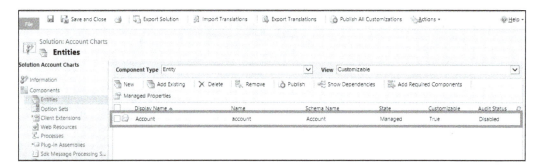

When we have our solution ready, we can just export and import it to other organizations.

As opposed to dashboards, we can export the personal charts and import them to other systems by using the **Export Chart** and **Import Chart** buttons that are available in the **Charts** tab of the entity's ribbon where we created a personal chart.

When exporting and importing charts to other organizations, it is very important that we check whether the versions of both organizations match to avoid issues. Be sure that we have the same rollup updates applied on both organizations.

To avoid overwriting other pieces of the entity (such as forms, ribbon customizations, and/or views) it is recommended that we unzip the solution ZIP file to our local drive and edit the `customization.xml` file by removing everything that is not related to the chart. Having only the chart, XML-related nodes will prevent us from overwriting other pieces of the entity that we don't want to touch on the target organization from where we will import the chart. To do this, we remove the `FormXml` nodes and the `RibbonDiffXml` nodes, leaving only the `Visualizations` node as follows:

```xml
<ImportExportXml xmlns:xsi="http://www.w3.org/2001/XMLSchema-
instance">
  <Entities>
    <Entity>
      <Name LocalizedName="Account" OriginalName="Account">Account</
Name>
      <ObjectTypeCode>1</ObjectTypeCode>
      <Visualizations>
        <visualization>
          <savedqueryvisualizationid>{B0F28CBB-B66E-E211-B407-
00155DFE7909}</savedqueryvisualizationid>
          <datadescription>
            <datadefinition>
              <fetchcollection>
                <fetch mapping="logical" aggregate="true" count="5">
                  <entity name="account">
                    <order alias="_CRMAutoGen_aggregate_column_Num_0"
descending="true" />
                    <attribute groupby="true" alias="_CRMAutoGen_
groupby_column_Num_0" name="address1_line1" />
                    <attribute alias="_CRMAutoGen_aggregate_column_
Num_0" name="name" aggregate="count" />
                  </entity>
                </fetch>
              </fetchcollection>
              <categorycollection>
                <category alias="_CRMAutoGen_groupby_column_Num_0">
                  <measurecollection>
                    <measure alias="_CRMAutoGen_aggregate_column_
Num_0" />
                  </measurecollection>
                </category>
              </categorycollection>
            </datadefinition>
          </datadescription>
          <presentationdescription>
            <Chart Palette="None" PaletteCustomColors="55,118,193;
197,56,52; 149,189,66; 117,82,160; 49,171,204; 255,136,35; 97,142,206;
209,98,96; 168,203,104; 142,116,178; 93,186,215; 255,155,83">
              <Series>
                <Series ChartType="Column" IsValueShownAsLabel="True"
Font="{0}, 9.5px" LabelForeColor="59, 59, 59" CustomProperties="PointW
idth=0.75, MaxPixelPointWidth=40"></Series>
```

```
            </Series>
            <ChartAreas>
              <ChartArea BorderColor="White"
BorderDashStyle="Solid">
                <AxisY LabelAutoFitMinFontSize="8"
TitleForeColor="59, 59, 59" TitleFont="{0}, 10.5px" LineColor="165,
172, 181" IntervalAutoMode="VariableCount">
                  <MajorGrid LineColor="239, 242, 246" />
                  <MajorTickMark LineColor="165, 172, 181" />
                  <LabelStyle Font="{0}, 10.5px" ForeColor="59, 59,
59" />
                </AxisY>
                <AxisX LabelAutoFitMinFontSize="8"
TitleForeColor="59, 59, 59" TitleFont="{0}, 10.5px" LineColor="165,
172, 181" IntervalAutoMode="VariableCount">
                  <MajorTickMark LineColor="165, 172, 181" />
                  <MajorGrid LineColor="Transparent" />
                  <LabelStyle Font="{0}, 10.5px" ForeColor="59, 59,
59" />
                </AxisX>
              </ChartArea>
            </ChartAreas>
            <Titles>
              <Title Alignment="TopLeft" DockingOffset="-3"
Font="{0}, 13px" ForeColor="59, 59, 59"></Title>
            </Titles>
            <Legends>
              <Legend Alignment="Center" LegendStyle="Table"
Docking="right" IsEquallySpacedItems="True" Font="{0}, 11px"
ShadowColor="0, 0, 0, 0" ForeColor="59, 59, 59" />
            </Legends>
          </Chart>
        </presentationdescription>
        <isdefault>0</isdefault>
        <LocalizedNames>
          <LocalizedName description="Top 5: Account Name by Address
1: Street 1" languagecode="1033" />
        </LocalizedNames>
        <IsCustomizable>1</IsCustomizable>
      </visualization>
    </Visualizations>
```

```
        </Entity>
    </Entities>
    <Roles></Roles>
    <Workflows></Workflows>
    <FieldSecurityProfiles></FieldSecurityProfiles>
    <Templates />
    <EntityMaps />
    <EntityRelationships />
    <OrganizationSettings />
    <optionsets />
    <Languages>
        <Language>1033</Language>
    </Languages>
</ImportExportXml>
```

Now, we want to export our chart as we want to distribute it as a commercial solution; so we would probably want to change the dashboard settings to not allow the external user to be able to customize it.

To do this, expand the entity where we have the chart, then click on **Charts**, select the chart we want to prevent users to customize, and click on **More Actions** then on **Managed properties**. Select **False** and click on **OK**.

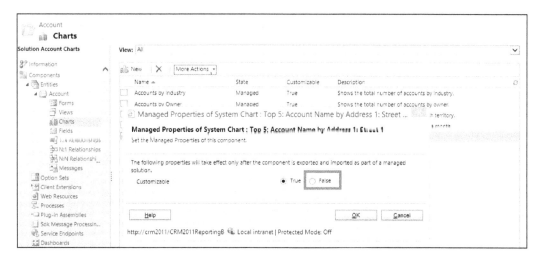

Charts internals

As we can see charts are stored in CRM as XML text. When a chart is exported, we can see the XML code under the `Visualizations` node. By looking at the XML code, we can make some other cool customizations that are not supported by using the standard chart editor.

For example, we could change the font size and color of the Y axis of the chart by modifying the `AxisY` node as follows:

```
<AxisY LabelAutoFitMinFontSize="8" TitleForeColor="255, 0, 0"
TitleFont="{0}, 20px" LineColor="165, 172, 181" IntervalAutoMode="Var
iableCount">
```

Save this change on the `Customization.Xml` file, compress the files again into a new ZIP file, and then import the solution back to our organization. We will see the chart displayed as follows:

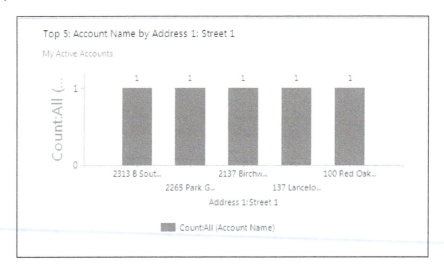

 To understand more about the Charts XML format go to http://msdn.microsoft.com/en-us/library/gg327901.aspx.

3D charts

Another thing we can do by modifying the XML code that we cannot do with the chart editor is enabling the 3D in the charts. Add the following code at the end of the `ChartArea` section to the same code as we used before:

```
<Area3DStyle Enable3D="True" LightStyle="Realistic" WallWidth="5"
IsRightAngleAxes="true" />
```

After making this change, create the ZIP file and import the solution again to CRM and we will see the following result:

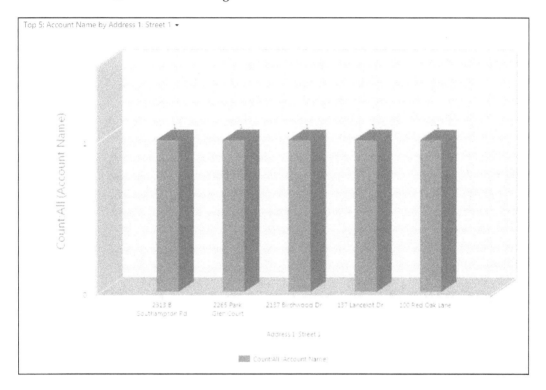

While the 3D charts are briefly documented in the CRM SDK, I'd like to include a reference to the article that Jukka Niiranen posted on this link, explaining the different parameters in detail:

http://niiranen.eu/crm/2010/10/turn-the-flat-dynamics-crm-2011-charts-into-3d/

Summary

In this chapter, we looked at how we can integrate a report in a CRM Dashboard, explained the Chart basics as well as the details of the charts, which is always a good option to display important information about the CRM system if we don't want to use reports.

In the next chapter, we are going to see how we can integrate a custom report with Dynamics CRM 2011 that can be created with ASP.NET or Silverlight. We will see sample code with early and late bindings and how to automate the SQL reporting services' report execution.

8
Advance Custom Reporting and Automation

In this chapter, we are going to see how we can integrate a custom report with Dynamics CRM 2011 that can be created with ASP.NET or Silverlight. We will see sample codes with early and late bindings and how to automate the SQL reporting services' report execution. This can be done either with the CRM web interface or using code to automate a report-generated file such as a PDF file.

The ASP.NET report

There might be different reasons why we can find some limitations with the reports created in **SQL Server Reporting Services** (**SSRS**); for example, using some dynamic controls, which are already available for ASP.NET and are not needed on an RDL report, might be a good reason to think about creating our own custom report in ASP.NET.

Open Visual Studio 2012 and create a new website application as shown in the following screenshot:

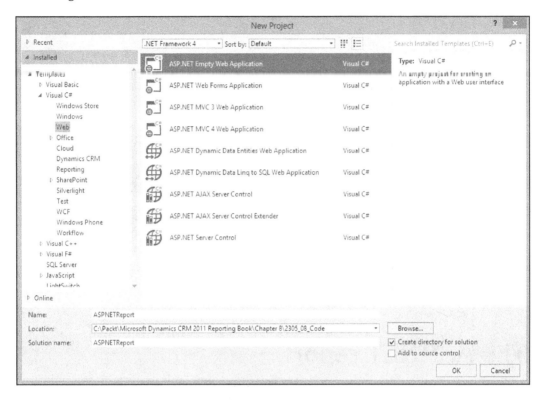

When working with ASP.NET, we will need to manage the Dynamics CRM connections and opt for one of the methods used to connect our controls with the CRM entities' data records. We can use early or late binding, which will be described in detail next.

When connecting custom applications to Dynamics CRM, it is always recommended to not go directly to the database; instead, it is better to use the native CRM WCF services that are exposed for any application integration we might need to build.

> Before starting to write any application, we will need to download the Microsoft CRM SDK from the Microsoft download site: http://www.microsoft.com/en-us/download/details. aspx?id=24004.

Late binding

Late binding means that we won't tighten our code with the CRM entities (either system or customs) to our ASP.NET solution, so we will discover the entities' names and fields at runtime. This method does not have IntelliSense, but it is more generic if our solution needs to be installed in different organizations where the number of entities can be unknown.

To use late binding we have two options:

- Add references to the `Microsoft.xrm.sdk.dll` and `Microsoft.crm.sdk.proxy.dll` assemblies that come with the CRM SDK in the `sdk\bin` folder
- Add a reference of the `organization.svc` service that is usually found at `http://servername/organization/XRMServices/2011/Organization.svc`

To be sure we use the right address, go to the CRM web interface, and perform the following steps:

1. Go to **Settings | Customizations | Developer Resources**.

   We will find the organization's service address there.

2. Copy that URL and create a web reference in our Visual Studio solution by right-clicking on the project's name and clicking on the **Add Service Reference...** menu option, as shown in the following screenshot:

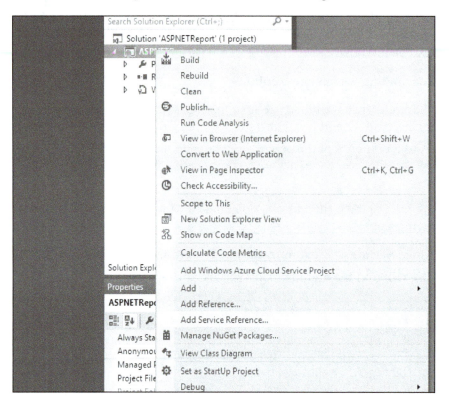

3. Paste the URL in the **Address** textbox appended with `?wsdl` and click on the **Go** button.

   We should see **OrganizationService** listed in the **Services** list.

4. Enter a good name for the namespace, such as `CrmService`.

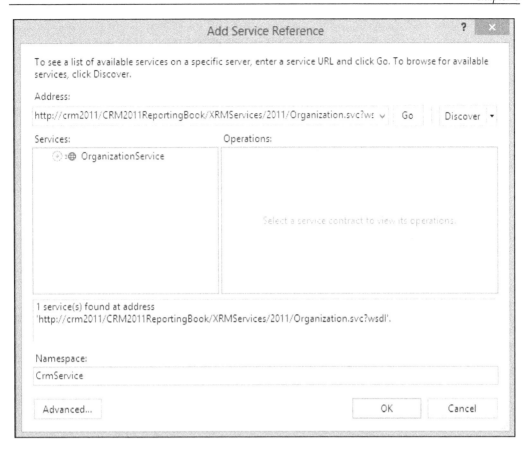

5. Click on **OK** to add the reference and we should see the service listed under **Services References**, as shown in the following screenshot:

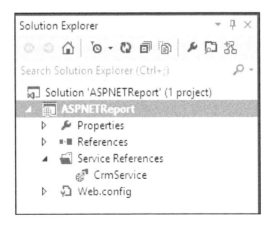

6. Create a new class named `CrmAccounts` and add the following code. As we can see, using late binding is great to use Fetch XML queries if we are familiar with this language:

```
using System.Data;
using ASPNETReport.CrmService;

namespace ASPNETReport
{
    public class CrmAccounts
    {
        private CrmService.OrganizationServiceClient client;
        public  CrmAccounts()
        {
            client = new CrmService.OrganizationServiceClient();
        }
        public DataTable GetAllAccounts()
        {
            DataTable accounts = new DataTable("Accounts");
            accounts.Columns.Add("name");
            accounts.Columns.Add("accountid");
            string fetchQuery = @"
                <fetch distinct='false' mapping='logical' >
                    <entity name='account'>
                        <attribute name='name' />
                        <attribute name='accountid' />
                    </entity>
                </fetch>";
            var fetchExpression = new FetchExpression();
            fetchExpression.Query = fetchQuery;

            EntityCollection crmaccounts = client.RetrieveMultiple(fetchExpression);
            foreach (var c in crmaccounts.Entities)
            {
                DataRow mRow = accounts.NewRow();
                mRow["name"] = c.Attributes[0].Value.ToString();
                mRow["accountid"] = c.Attributes[1].Value.ToString();

                accounts.Rows.Add(mRow);
            }
            return accounts;
        }
    }
}
```

We can see more samples of late binding operations by referring to the CRM SDK in the `sdk\samplecode\cs\generalprogramming\latebound` folder.

7. Now add a page to our solution and then a `GridView` control, and choose a data source by selecting the **Object Data Source** type.

8. Enter `CRMObjectDataSource` as the name for the data source.

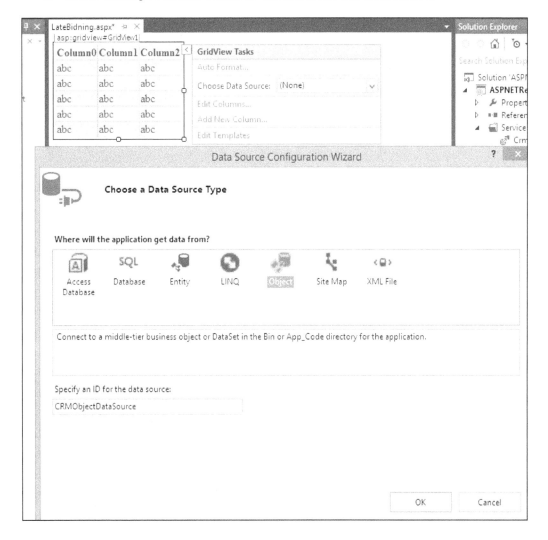

9. Click on **OK** to continue.

10. Select the **ASPNETReport.CrmAccounts** object type. If we don't see this object type, it is because we need to rebuild our solution first. Then click on **Next** to continue.

11. Select the **GetAllAccounts(), returns DataTable** method and click on **Finish**.

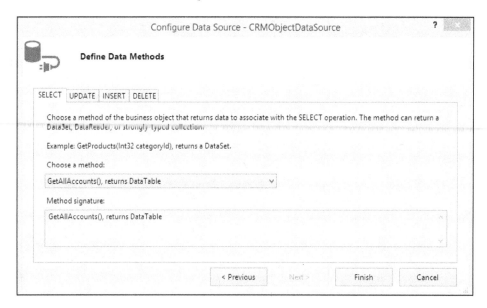

12. Press *F5* to run our solution, and we should see the report's result as shown in the following screenshot:

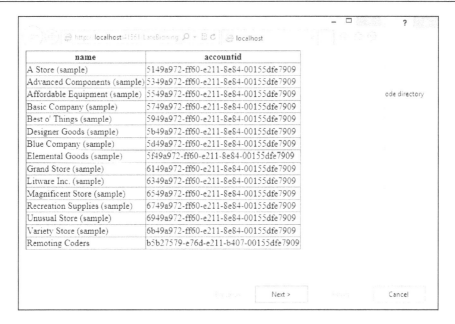

Early binding

As opposed to late binding, early binding will allow us to know the entities' names and fields at development time, so we can validate our code better at compile time. It also adds IntelliSense, so we can easily find the fields we need to use for avoiding misspellings in the code that would then fail at runtime, like we would be facing with late binding.

To use early binding, we will need to create the entity model by using the CrmSvcUtil.exe tool that comes with Dynamics CRM SDK that can be found in the sdk\bin folder.

This is a command-prompt application, and to run this tool, we will need to pass the CRM URL containing the organization name, shown as follows:

```
CrmSvcUtil.exe /url:http://crm2011/CRM2011ReportingBook/
XRMServices/2011/Organization.svc /out:crmcode.cs
```

For more information about the CrmSvcUtil.exe command-line parameters, refer to the MSDN article found at http://msdn.microsoft.com/en-in/library/gg695820.aspx.

Depending on whether our CRM organization is located in CRM Online or in an on-premise environment with Claims-based authentication enabled, we will need to pass the credentials (the username and password) as parameters as well.

Now we need to add this generated code (crmcode.cs) to our Visual Studio project.

If we try to build the solution, we will get a lot of errors. This is because we also need to add the microsoft.xrm.sdk.dll assembly reference that can be found in the sdk\bin folder under the CRM's **Software Development Kit (SDK)**.

Now in order to use early binding, we only need to replace the code that we put in the CrmAccounts.cs file with the following code:

```
using System;
using System.Data;
using System.ServiceModel.Description;
using Microsoft.Xrm.Sdk;
using Microsoft.Xrm.Sdk.Query;

namespace ASPNETReport
{
    public class CrmAccounts
    {
        private Microsoft.Xrm.Sdk.Client.OrganizationServiceProxy
client;
        public CrmAccounts()
        {
            ClientCredentials credentials = new ClientCredentials();
            credentials.Windows.ClientCredential = System.Net.
CredentialCache.DefaultNetworkCredentials;
            client = new Microsoft.Xrm.Sdk.Client.
OrganizationServiceProxy(
                new Uri("http://crm2011/CRM2011ReportingBook/
XRMServices/2011/Organization.svc"),
                new Uri("http://crm2011/CRM2011ReportingBook/
XRMServices/2011/Organization.svc"), credentials, null);
        }
```

```
public DataTable GetAllAccounts()
{
    DataTable accounts = new DataTable("Accounts");
    accounts.Columns.Add("name");
    accounts.Columns.Add("accountid");
    string fetchQuery = @"
        <fetch distinct='false' mapping='logical' >
            <entity name='account'>
                <attribute name='name'   />
                <attribute name='accountid'   />
            </entity>
        </fetch>";
    var fetchExpression = new FetchExpression(fetchQuery);

    DataCollection<Entity> crmaccounts =
(DataCollection<Entity>)client.RetrieveMultiple(fetchExpression).
Entities;
    foreach (Entity c in crmaccounts)
    {
        Account myAccount = c.ToEntity<Account>();
        DataRow mRow = accounts.NewRow();
        mRow["name"] = myAccount.Name;
        mRow["accountid"] = myAccount.AccountId.Value.
ToString();

        accounts.Rows.Add(mRow);
    }
    return accounts;
    }
}
}
```

 We can see more samples of late binding operations by referring to the CRM SDK in the sdk\samplecode\cs\ generalprogramming\earlybound folder.

Building and running this code will produce the same results as the late binding sample code.

CRM integration

Now to see our Custom ASP.NET report integrated with Dynamics CRM, go to the CRM web interface and click on **Reports | New**.

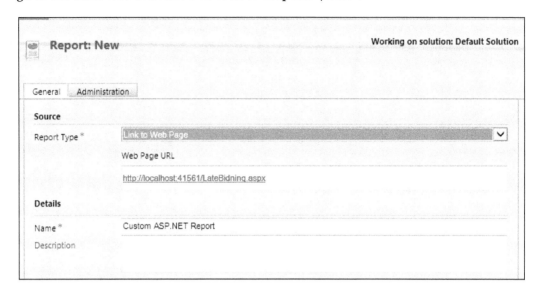

In the **Report Type** drop-down list, select the **Link to Web Page** option and enter the ASP.NET report's URL in the **Web Page URL** textbox. In this sample, we used a localhost to test the development report, but we will need to provide a real URL so that other users can also see this report. We will need to host the ASP.NET application on an external IIS website.

Enter a name for our report and click on **Save** to close this dialog. Our report will be available in the reports view. When we run our report, it will look the same as when we run it from Visual Studio.

Silverlight reports

Silverlight is another option for creating dynamic reports that can be updated automatically, for example, by using a timer; this is a perfect method to create a monitoring console on a Dynamics CRM Dashboard, although Silverlight is a technology that is going to be deprecated by Microsoft, and there are not going to be more versions. The latest version (Version 5) has been announced to be the last one, as it is going to be replaced by HTML 5. Microsoft is going to support Silverlight for another 10 years.

Silverlight is a subset of **Windows Presentation Foundation** (**WPF**) and is created specifically to be used on a web browser. The Adobe Flash player works in a similar way. Silverlight also uses the **Application Extensibility Markup Language** (**AXML**) as the WPF does. This technology allows a vectored representation of any control that can be zoomed, without losing the aspect, and also allows the creation of great animations that can be easily done using Microsoft Expression Blend.

When working with Silverlight, we need to keep in mind that all the web services' calls to the Dynamics CRM web services must be asynchronous. For this reason, choosing a good methodology to develop our Silverlight applications is highly recommended, as we will see next.

MVVM

When working with Silverlight, it is recommended to adopt a good methodology to develop applications. One of the best methodologies I have found is **Model View ViewModel** (**MVVM**). It is a three-layer methodology, where the Model is equivalent to the data access layer, the View is equivalent to the user presentation layer, and the ViewModel is equivalent to the business rules layer that connects the Model and the Views, so that these two layers don't need to know what they do. This methodology allows the developer to create a loosely coupled application.

There are several templates for MVVM available on the Internet to use; I recommend using MVVM Light, which can be downloaded from CodePlex by going to http://mvvmlight.codeplex.com/.

Create a new Visual Studio 2012 project using the MVVM Light project template as shown in the following screenshot:

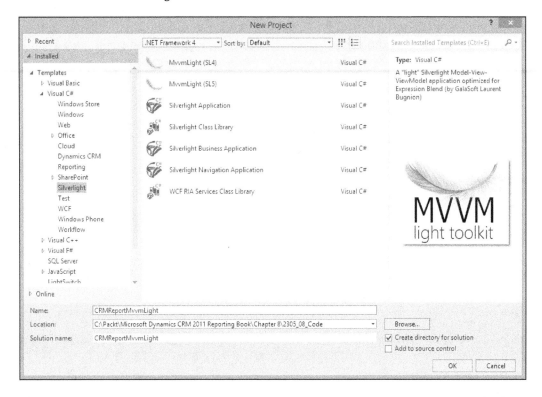

Add the CRM Service reference in the same way as we did for the ASP.NET solution. This reference will need to slightly modify the code, and since this sample also requires lots of lines of code, we will explain the most important parts. Also, we can download the full working code from the Packt site.

Open the view, which is the \MainPage.xaml file. We just replace the TextBlock control with the DataGrid control so that we can display the record results as follows:

```
<sdk:DataGrid ItemsSource="{Binding CRMAccounts}"
AutoGenerateColumns="False" />
```

In the ViewModel\MainViewModel.cs page, put the following in the constructor to connect the view with the model:

```
public MainViewModel(IDataService dataService)
        {
            _dataService = dataService;
            CRMAccounts = _dataService.GetEntities((item, excep)
=>{});
        }
```

The `Model\DataService.cs` file is where we actually connect to the CRM service to perform the fetch query with the following code:

```
public ObservableCollection<EntityClass> GetEntities(Action<Ob
servableCollection<EntityClass>, Exception> callback)
    {
        try
        {
            _entities = new ObservableCollection<EntityClass>();
            OrganizationServiceClient client =
(OrganizationServiceClient)GetConnection();
            string fetchQuery = @"
            <fetch distinct='false' mapping='logical' >
                <entity name='account'>
                    <attribute name='name'  />
                    <attribute name='accountid'  />
                </entity>
            </fetch>";
            var fetchexp = new FetchExpression();
            fetchexp.Query = fetchQuery;

            client.RetrieveMultipleCompleted += (s, response) =>
            {

                ObservableCollection<Entity> entitylist = new
ObservableCollection<Entity>();
                foreach (Entity ent in response.Result.Entities)
                {
                    KeyValuePairOfstringanyType keyValue = ent.
Attributes.Where(a => a.key == "name").First();
                    KeyValuePairOfstringanyType keyValue2 = ent.
Attributes.Where(a => a.key == "accountid").First();

                    _entities.Add(new EntityClass() { Name =
keyValue.value.ToString(), AccountId = keyValue2.value.ToString() });
                }

                if (_fetchCallback != null)
                {
                    _fetchCallback(entitylist);
                }
            };

            client.RetrieveMultipleAsync(fetchexp);
            return _entities;
```

```
    }
    catch (FaultException<OrganizationServiceFault> ex)
    {
        throw ex;
    }
}
```

The result of this solution should be similar to the following screenshot:

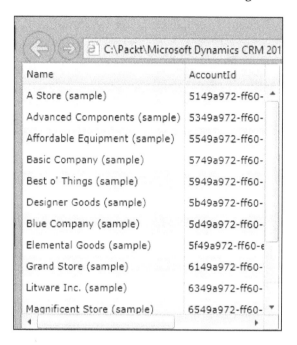

The deployment of the Silverlight report can be done in the same way we did for the ASP.NET report. We can also install the .xap file as a CRM web resource, which will avoid us to have a different web server setup. This way the report will run inside the CRM environment; this is especially helpful if we are on a CRM online environment.

Basic report automation

We can automate a report to be run automatically at specific dates/times by using the report scheduling; this will help to improve the report performance while having the report ready for the user whenever he needs it. The quickest and easiest way is by creating a report snapshot through the report scheduling directly from the Dynamics CRM interface, as we will see next.

Report scheduling

Dynamics CRM 2011 has some native features that allow us to automate the SSRS reports that we create with either the CRM Report Wizard or with Visual Studio by configuring an automated run schedule. This feature is available in the **Reports** ribbon in the **Actions** group under the **Schedule Report** button, as shown in the following screenshot:

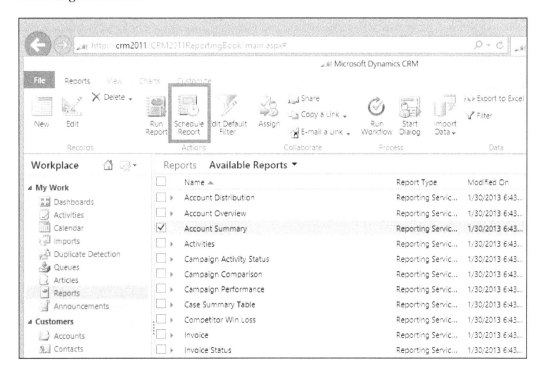

When we click on this button, we will be presented with a dialog that will have two options:

- **On demand**
- **On a schedule**

These options will generate snapshots of the report whenever we specify; if we select **On a schedule**, we will be able to specify a recurrence period where we want the report to be run. This is perfect for reports that take a long time to complete. So we can schedule them to run every week and have them completed by the time we need the information.

The following screenshot shows how this dialog is presented to the user:

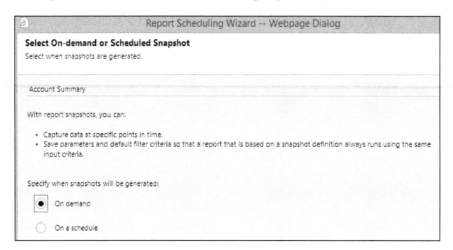

If we select the **On a schedule** option, we will be able to set the frequency when we want the snapshots to be created.

The available options are as follows:

- **Once**
- **Hourly**
- **Daily**
- **Weekly**
- **Monthly**

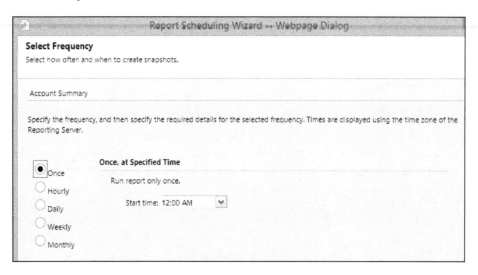

Depending on the option we select, we will be presented with different settings. The following is how the different options look if we select **Hourly**:

If we select **Daily**, different options are available as shown in the following screenshot:

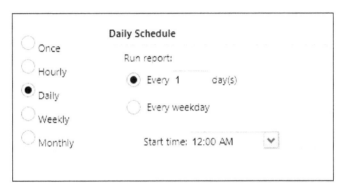

If we select **Weekly**, we will be able to select the number of weeks and days we want the report to run:

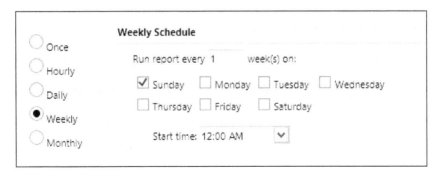

By selecting **Monthly**, we will be able to select the number of days of a month or the number of weeks of a month, as well as the time where we want the report to be scheduled:

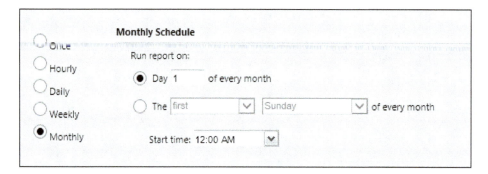

Then, depending on the report we selected, we will be presented with a dialog from where we will be able to predefine the report filter criteria. In our sample, we selected the **Account Summary** report, so we will see the following filters:

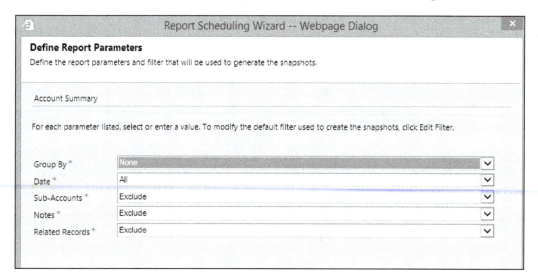

Click on **Next** to continue, and we will be presented with a summary dialog to confirm:

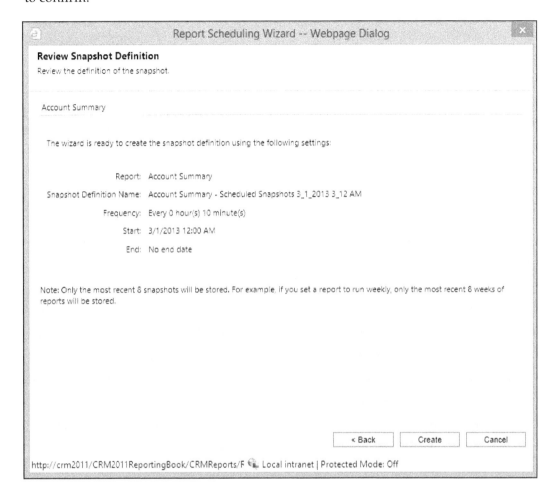

Click on **Create** to complete the wizard; this process might take a few minutes to complete. When it finishes, we will see the following dialog:

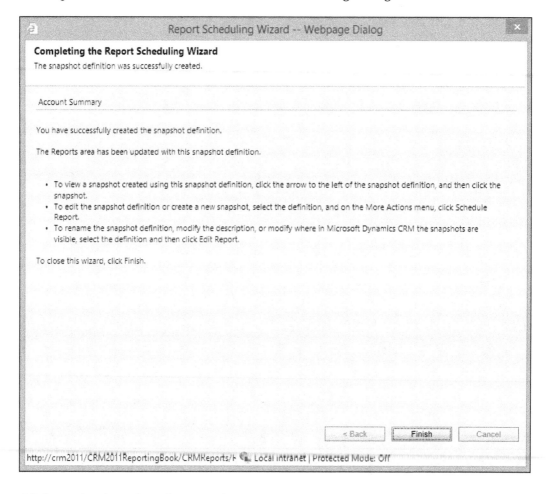

Click on **Finish** to close the wizard. Once the report snapshots are created, we will see them in the report's gridview as follows:

By opening these reports, the gridview will run much faster than the original one, as it will show only a snapshot of the report that was generated at that date and time when the report was scheduled.

To change the frequency of the scheduled report, click on the scheduled report that was created, and click on the **Schedule Report** button from the ribbon again.

Clicking on the arrow near the checkbox will show us the snapshots of the report that ran previously:

Clicking on any of the snapshot's lines will show us the report with the results that were collected at that time, and of course, the report will be displayed much faster because of that.

Advanced report automation (programmatically)

If we want to run a CRM report automatically from a custom application such as a Windows or ASP.NET web application, we can do it programmatically as we will see in this chapter.

Before creating a solution in Visual Studio, we need to be sure that we can access our report externally by publishing it for external use. To do that we need to go to the CRM web interface and then to the reports. Find the report we want to automate and click on the **Edit** button from the ribbon. In our example we will use **Account Summary** (out of the box) report. When the **Edit report** dialog is open, go to the **Actions** menu and select the **Publish Report for External Use** menu option.

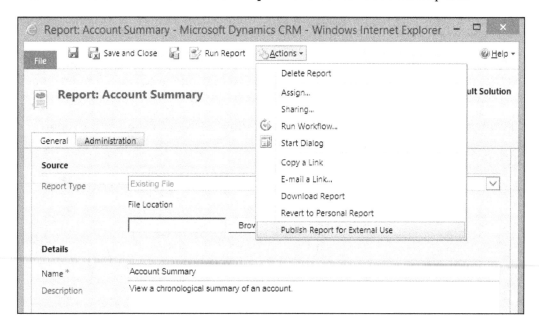

Clicking this option will not return any resultant message. To check whether it is published successfully, we will need to run the Report Manager web application and then go to the folder of our organization. There we will need to validate if we have a report with the report name there, as shown in the following screenshot:

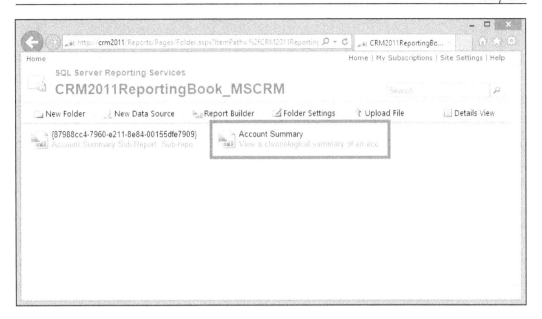

In our example, we will use a web application to create our Visual Studio solution. We will need to add the following references to our project:

- **Microsoft.ReportViewer.Common**
- **Microsoft.ReportViewer.Webforms**

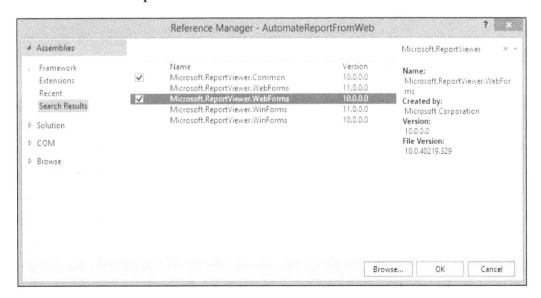

Depending on the SSRS version, we might need to use the 10.0.0.0
Version for SQL 2008 R2 or 11.0.0.0 for SQL Server 2012. Using
the 10.0.0.0 Version will also work on SQL 2012, while the 11.0.0.0
Version won't work on SQL 2008 R2.

Add a web page to our project with the name of `Default.aspx` and add a button
to it named `RunCRMReportButton`. In the `click` event write the following code:

```
protected void RunCRMReportButton_Click(object sender, EventArgs e)
{
        Warning[] warnings;
        string mimeType;
        string encoding;
        string extension;
        string[] streams;
        byte[] bytes;

        string reportTempId = Guid.NewGuid().ToString();
        string tempDirectory = Server.MapPath("~/");
        string destinationPath = tempDirectory + "Temp\\" +
reportTempId + ".pdf";

        ReportViewer myReportViewer = new ReportViewer();

        myReportViewer.ProcessingMode = ProcessingMode.Remote;
        myReportViewer.ServerReport.ReportServerUrl = new
Uri("http://crm2011/reportserver");
        myReportViewer.ServerReport.ReportServerCredentials = new
ReportServerCredentials();
        myReportViewer.ServerReport.ReportPath = "/
CRM2011ReportingBook_MSCRM/Account Summary";

        ReportParameterInfoCollection parameters2 =
myReportViewer.ServerReport.GetParameters();
        ReportParameter[] parameters = new
ReportParameter[parameters2.Count];
        int counter = 0;

        foreach (ReportParameterInfo item in parameters2)
        {
            if (item.Name == "GroupBy")
            {
                parameters[counter] = new ReportParameter(item.
Name, item.Values[0]); //"Owner");
```

```
            }
            else
            {
                parameters[counter] = new ReportParameter(item.
Name, item.Values[0]);
            }
            counter++;
        }

    // Sets the report parameters
        myReportViewer.ServerReport.SetParameters(parameters);

    // Executes the report and exports it to PDF format
        bytes = myReportViewer.ServerReport.Render("PDF", null,
out mimeType, out encoding, out extension, out streams, out warnings);

        // Saves the report to a file in the local hard drive
FileInfo myFile = new FileInfo(destinationPath);

        FileStream stream = File.OpenWrite(destinationPath);
        stream.Write(bytes, 0, bytes.Length);
        stream.Close();
    }
```

The ReportServerCredentials class will be coded as follows:

```
using System.Configuration;

namespace AutomateReportFromWeb
{
    class ReportServerCredentials : Microsoft.Reporting.WebForms.
IReportServerCredentials
    {
        private string _domain;
        private string _userName;
        private string _password;
        private string _userName2;
        private string _domain2;
        private string _password2;

        public ReportServerCredentials()
        {
            _userName = ConfigurationManager.AppSettings["username"];
            _password = ConfigurationManager.AppSettings["password"];
            _domain = ConfigurationManager.AppSettings["domain"];
```

```
        }

        public ReportServerCredentials(string userName, string
password, string domain)
        {
            _userName2 = userName;
            _password2 = password;
            _domain2 = domain;
        }


        public System.Security.Principal.WindowsIdentity
ImpersonationUser
        {
            get
            {
                return null;
            }
        }


        public System.Net.ICredentials NetworkCredentials
        {
            get
            {
                return new System.Net.NetworkCredential(_userName,
_password, _domain);
                //return System.Net.CredentialCache.
DefaultCredentials;
            }
        }


        public bool GetFormsCredentials(out System.Net.Cookie
authCookie, out string userName, out string password, out string
authority)
        {
            // Do not use forms credentials to authenticate.
            authCookie = null;
            authority = null;
            password = _password2;
            userName = _userName2;
            return false;
        }
    }
}
```

Summary

In this chapter, we looked at how we can integrate a custom ASP.NET or Silverlight application to show a dynamic or more sophisticated report inside Dynamics CRM 2011. We looked at the different ways to bind the CRM data by using early or late binding methods, and finally, we looked at some ways to automate SSRS reports by either using scheduling or by automating the export file generation with code.

In the next chapter, we are going to see how we can troubleshoot errors that might happen in our reports in Dynamics CRM 2011. We are also going to review the best practices of report development and deployment, as well as some techniques to improve the performance of our reports.

9
Failure Recovery and Best Practices

In this chapter, we are going to see how we can troubleshoot errors that might occur on our reports in Dynamics CRM 2011. We are also going to review the best practices of report development and deployment, as well as some techniques to improve the performance of reports.

Common failures in SSR authentication

Dynamics CRM uses its own authentication method that can be either of the following:

- Windows authentication
- Claims-based authentication
- Office 365 for CRM online

Once the user is authenticated on CRM, we don't want to request authentication again to run a report that is running on a separate server; that is why the CRM Reporting extensions need to be installed. What happens is that the CRM needs to authenticate the user against SQL Reporting Service in order to allow report execution. This process is also called a double-hop authentication. If this is not properly configured, we might receive an error, **The report cannot be displayed. (rsProcessingAborted)**, as shown in the following screenshot:

Sometimes, we might also get an error such as **The report cannot be displayed. (rsInvalidDataSourceReference)**. If this happens, we need to be sure that our report is pointing to the right data source. When developing reports with Visual Studio (or with Report Builder), the data source might point to a wrong place. To validate this, go to the Report Manager Web interface (usually found at http://reportservername/reports/) and find the folder of your CRM organization.

Reports can be configured to be viewed either by the entire organization or by an individual who is the owner of the report. This can be set by clicking on the report and then the **Edit** button from the ribbon and then switching to the **Administration** tab.

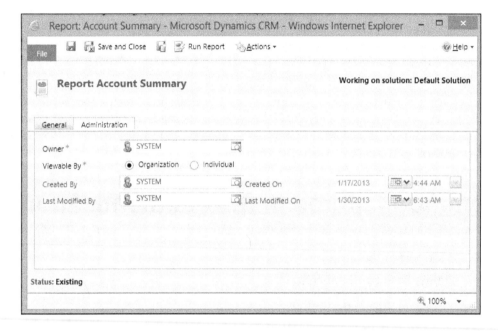

If a user cannot see the report, make sure that this setting is not set to individual. If for some reason we don't want everybody to be able to see and run a report, we can set it to be viewed individually and then share it with a user or team.

Tracing

Tracing is a method to record everything a process does in a verbose mode so we can see exactly what a process is doing. There are different components that we might require to see and read the trace logs if the error description we are receiving is not very useful. For example, getting an error such as **Generic SQL Error occur** is not helpful, and we need to discover what is happening behind the scenes to understand what is causing the problem.

Enabling CRM Trace

CRM Trace can be enabled by touching some registry keys on the server as explained in this KB (`http://support.microsoft.com/kb/907490`). However, the safest and easiest way to enable the trace is by using Diagnostics Tool for Microsoft Dynamics CRM 2011 that my fellow Microsoft MVP, *Tanguy Touzard* created and published on CodePlex. This tool can be downloaded from `http://crmdiagtool2011.codeplex.com/`, and when we run it, we will see a window similar to the following screenshot:

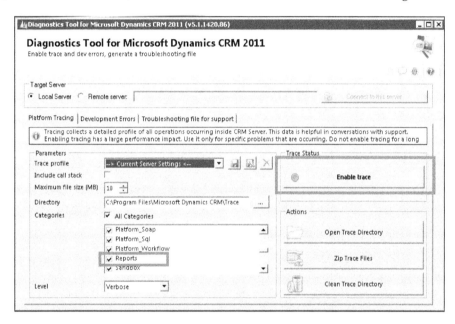

Be sure to have the **Reports** option selected, and click on the **Enable trace** button to let the trace start. Once we have enabled the trace, we can perform the steps to reproduce the error. When we get the error, we can get back to this tool and click on the **Open Trace Directory** button to see the trace files.

> It is recommended to clean the trace directory first by clicking on the **Clean Trace Directory** button, in case we had old trace files.

Name	Date modified	Type	Size
CRM2011-ReportingServicesService-bin-20130228-1.log	2/28/2013 9:20 PM	Text Document	9 KB
CRM2011-CrmAsyncService(3272#B84B78F6)-bin-20130228-1.log	2/28/2013 9:20 PM	Text Document	0 KB
CRM2011-Microsoft.Crm.Sandbox.HostService-bin-20130228-1.log	2/28/2013 9:20 PM	Text Document	0 KB
CRM2011-w3wp(5440#5576A618)-CRMWeb-20130228-1.log	2/28/2013 9:20 PM	Text Document	2 KB
CRM2011-CrmAsyncService(1988#F6334FA5)-bin-20130228-1.log	2/28/2013 9:20 PM	Text Document	0 KB

The names of the files will depend on the date and server where we ran the trace, but the important ones to look for are the ones that contain the `w3wp` and `ReportingServicesService` trace files in the filename.

Here is an example of the `w3wp` trace file:

```
# CRM Tracing Version 2.0
# LocalTime: 2013-02-28 21:20:37.000
# Categories: Reports.*:Verbose
# CallStackOn: No
# ComputerName: CRM2011
# CRMVersion: 5.0.9900.1010
# DeploymentType: OnPremise
# ScaleGroup:
# ServerRole: AppServer, AsyncService, DiscoveryService,
ApiServer, HelpServer, DeploymentService, SandboxServer,
DeploymentManagementTools

[2013-02-28 21:20:37.000] Process: w3wp |Organization:7308a7ba-
7760-e211-8e84-00155dfe7909 |Thread:   59 |Category: Reports |User:
871cc4fa-03fd-495a-930d-bb5c1c2bec61 |Level: Verbose |ReqId: 2a46eef4-
cb08-4104-a61c-8512cf8e1450 | ReportServer.IsDataConnectorConfigured
ilOffset = 0x0
>Calling ReportingService.GetDataSourceContents on: /
SharedReports/5.0.xxxx/MSCRM_FetchDataSource.
[2013-02-28 21:20:37.344] Process: w3wp |Organization:7308a7ba-
7760-e211-8e84-00155dfe7909 |Thread:   59 |Category: Reports
|User: 871cc4fa-03fd-495a-930d-bb5c1c2bec61 |Level: Verbose
|ReqId: 2a46eef4-cb08-4104-a61c-8512cf8e1450 | RuntimeReportServer.
IsDataConnectorConfigured  ilOffset = 0xA9
>Calling ReportingService.GetDataSourceContents on: /
CRM2011ReportingBook MSCRM/CustomReports/MSCRM_FetchDataSource.
[2013-02-28 21:20:37.375] Process: w3wp |Organization:7308a7ba-
7760-e211-8e84-00155dfe7909 |Thread:   59 |Category: Reports |User:
871cc4fa-03fd-495a-930d-bb5c1c2bec61 |Level: Verbose |ReqId: 2a46eef4-
cb08-4104-a61c-8512cf8e1450 | ReportServer.IsDataConnectorConfigured
ilOffset = 0x0
>Calling ReportingService.GetDataSourceContents on: /
SharedReports/5.0.xxxx/MSCRM_DataSource.
[2013-02-28 21:20:37.391] Process: w3wp |Organization:7308a7ba-
7760-e211-8e84-00155dfe7909 |Thread:   59 |Category: Reports
|User: 871cc4fa-03fd-495a-930d-bb5c1c2bec61 |Level: Verbose
|ReqId: 2a46eef4-cb08-4104-a61c-8512cf8e1450 | RuntimeReportServer.
IsDataConnectorConfigured  ilOffset = 0xA9
>Calling ReportingService.GetDataSourceContents on: /
CRM2011ReportingBook_MSCRM/CustomReports/MSCRM_DataSource.
```

To help read and work with these trace logfiles, we can download and use the CRM Trace Log Viewer tool that can be downloaded from `http://www.stunnware.com/crm2/topic.aspx?id=tracelogviewer`.

And here is an example of the `ReportingServicesService` logfile; this is the file where we will find all report-related information:

```
# CRM Tracing Version 2.0
# LocalTime: 2013-02-28 21:20:38.297
# Categories: Reports.*:Verbose
# CallStackOn: No
# ComputerName: CRM2011
# CRMVersion: 5.0.9900.1010
# DeploymentType: OnPremise
# ScaleGroup:
# ServerRole: AppServer, AsyncService, DiscoveryService,
ApiServer, HelpServer, DeploymentService, SandboxServer,
DeploymentManagementTools

[2013-02-28 21:20:38.297] Process:ReportingServicesService
|Organization:00000000-0000-0000-0000-000000000000 |Thread:   29
|Category: Reports |User: 00000000-0000-0000-0000-000000000000 |Level:
Info |ReqId:  | DataExtensionConnectionBase.ValidateCaller  ilOffset =
0x5
>Validating immediate caller.
[2013-02-28 21:20:39.312] Process:ReportingServicesService
|Organization:00000000-0000-0000-0000-000000000000 |Thread:   29
|Category: Reports |User: 00000000-0000-0000-0000-000000000000 |Level:
Info |ReqId:  | DataExtensionConnectionBase.ValidateCaller  ilOffset =
0xA4
>Immediate caller NT AUTHORITY\NETWORK SERVICE validated successfully.
[2013-02-28 21:20:39.312] Process:ReportingServicesService
|Organization:00000000-0000-0000-0000-000000000000 |Thread:   29
|Category: Reports |User: 00000000-0000-0000-0000-000000000000 |Level:
Info |ReqId:  | <>c__DisplayClass1.<Open>b__0  ilOffset = 0x3B
>Validating calling user.
[2013-02-28 21:20:39.359] Process:ReportingServicesService
|Organization:00000000-0000-0000-0000-000000000000 |Thread:   29
|Category: Reports |User: 00000000-0000-0000-0000-000000000000 |Level:
Info |ReqId:  | DataExtensionConnectionBase.ValidateUser  ilOffset =
0x4C
>Calling user S-1-5-20 validated successfully.
[2013-02-28 21:20:39.750] Process:ReportingServicesService
|Organization:00000000-0000-0000-0000-000000000000 |Thread:   29
|Category: Reports |User: 00000000-0000-0000-0000-000000000000 |Level:
Info |ReqId:  | DataExtensionConnectionBase.ValidateCaller  ilOffset =
0x5
```

Looking at this last trace file, we will be able to determine if there is any problem with the authentication between the CRM server and SQL Reporting Services. If we see the word error in this file, it will mean that we have a problem and we need to look at the details to be able to solve it.

Using SQL Trace

Using SQL Trace is good if we are using T-SQL sentences on our report. To trace SQL, we need to use SQL Server Profiler that is usually installed with the SQL Server development tools.

 Be careful when using the trace tools as they are heavily consumed resources. Also, we need to make sure that we turn them on when we need them to troubleshoot a problem. Do not forget to disable them when we are done or the whole server performance and user experience will be affected.

When we run this application, we will see the following window:

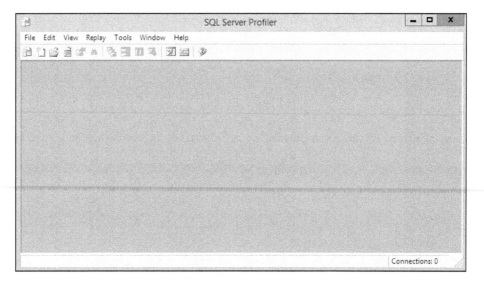

 This is a tool we will find on any version of SQL Server (from 2005 to 2012) that look very similar, so the configuration and results are the same regardless of the version of SQL Server we are using.

Follow these steps to trace SQL:

1. To start tracing SQL, go to the **File** menu and then click on the **New Trace…** option.

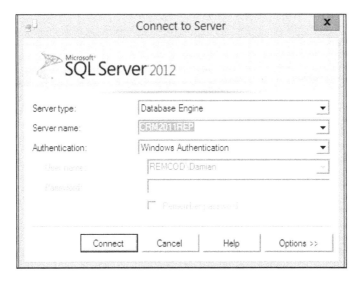

2. Select **Database Engine** in the **Server type** drop-down list and then select the database's server name and authentication. Then, click on the **Connect** button.

    The **Trace Properties** window will appear, allowing us to set a name for our trace as well as to select the template we want to use from one of the following predefined templates:

    °   Blank

    °   SP_Counts

    °   Standard

    °   TSQL

    °   TSQL_Duration

    °   TSQL_Locks

    °   TSQL_Reply

    °   TSQL_SPs

    °   Tuning

The Tuning template is the one that is used by the Database Tuning Advisor tool, which is also installed within SQL Server. We can read more about this tool at http://msdn.microsoft.com/en-us/library/ ms173494(v=sql.105).aspx.

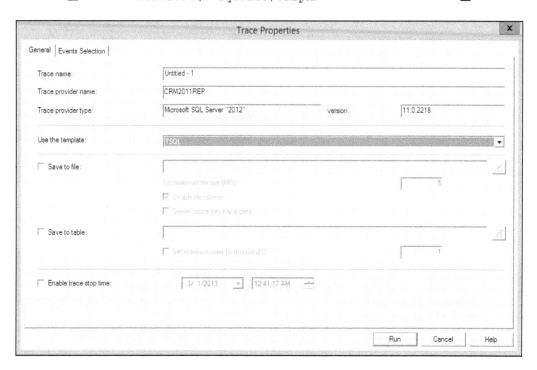

3. As an example, in the **Use the template** option select **TSQ** and then click on the **Events Selection** tab.

We will be presented with a predefined set of events and columns that will be specified in the template we selected. From here, we will be able to select the columns for each event in which we are interested in seeing the trace log result.

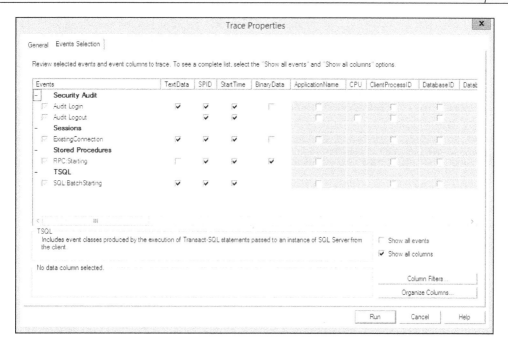

4. Select **Show all columns** to be able to select other columns such as **DatabaseName** and **LoginName**. We can optionally check the **Show all events** checkbox if we are interested in tracking other events not displayed by default on this template.

5. It is also good to filter the trace to show only the events of the CRM database. So to do this, click on the **Column Filters** button.

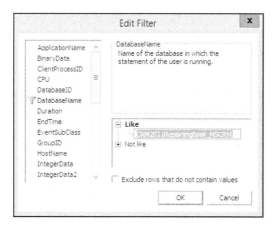

6. Click on **DatabaseName** and enter your CRM database name in the **Like** node.

7. Click on **OK** to close this dialog and then click on **Run** to start the trace.

We will see that all the TSQL sentences are flowing to SQL Server in real time; we can also pause and restart the trace at any time as well as clear the trace grid. If the trace log is too big, we can always go back to the properties to remove any unnecessary events or columns so we can easily identify the event and column we need to troubleshoot for our problem. The tools also allow us to search strings, so we don't need to read every line of the log if we are looking for a specific table or field.

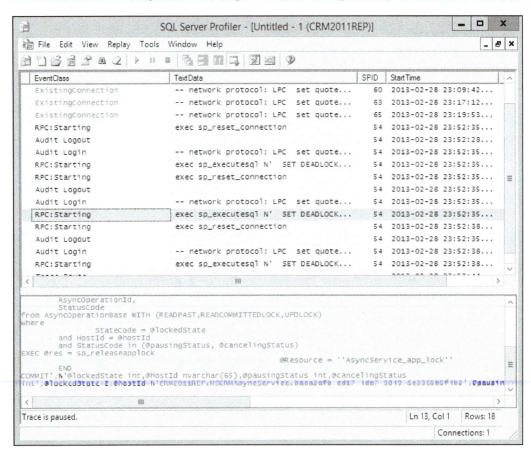

Selecting any row from the grid will show us the complete sentence that we can use to copy and paste; for example, we can copy and paste into SQL Server Management Studio to test the query ourselves in case we don't get the expected results or get an error.

Report development best practices

Use SQL server queries when possible; their performance is better than the Fetch XML queries. When using SQL queries, use stored procedures. They are precompiled in SQL Server and perform better than a query embedded in a report that needs to be interpreted and compiled every time we run the report.

We can also improve the performance of our SQL queries by looking at the execution plan of the query in SQL Server Management Studio.

This is something that can be enabled by clicking on the icon called **Display Estimated Execution Plan**, as shown in the following screenshot:

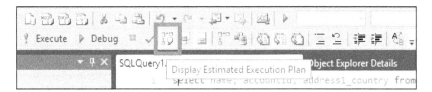

With this feature enabled, executing the query will suggest the indexes we might need to create to speed our query, as shown in the following screenshot:

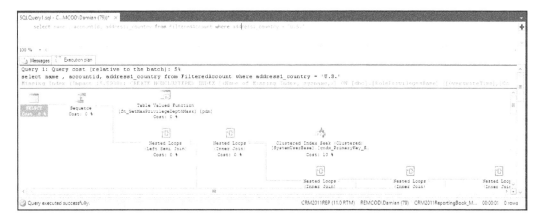

Creating indexes as this tool suggests will improve query performance a lot. For more information about working with this tool, go to `http://msdn.microsoft.com/en-us/library/ms190402.aspx`.

Be careful when creating lots of indexes as they can be counterproductive as they are good for queries but slower for inserts/updates and deletes.

Let's start our report by exporting one of the predefined, out-of-the box reports that comes with CRM 2011; they will have the properties that CRM will need already set. So, it will save us some time on report development, plus we will get the CRM 2011 report layout and its look and feel.

When we are done with our report development in SQL Reporting Services either using Visual Studio or Wizards, it is good practice to always validate how it looks when exporting the report to PDF. Many times, I have seen reports being returned back to developers because the exported PDF looks very bad. This happens especially when using grids that are split into separate pages.

When using date/time fields, we must be sure to validate our display with the right time for the time zone we are in. Most times, we get the time in GTM 0 when we are actually in a different time zone. So, the users will see the wrong date and time on the reports if we don't take care of this.

 We can read more about the best practices for reports with CRM at http://msdn.microsoft.com/en-us/library/gg334654.aspx.

Report deployment best practices

When we develop reports with Visual Studio, it is recommended to use a source control application system such as **Team Foundation Server** (**TFS**) so we can control the different changes we take with the versions.

If we create the reports with CRM Report Wizard, we can always get the generated RDL file by downloading it as explained in the *Using Visual Studio* recipe of *Chapter 3, Creating Your First Report in CRM*. So, we can store the file on a source control system such as TFS.

We can also use a tool such as reportsync that can be downloaded from https://code.google.com/p/reportsync/ and will help us get all the report files from SQL Reporting Services easily. It will also help us to synchronize our development environment with our production environment.

When deploying reports to other systems, try to always use CRM solutions that only include the reports we want to deploy and nothing else; this means that we should not include any entity or web resource within our reports so as to guarantee that the reports are easily categorized.

Improving the performance of reports

Once we have deployed our reports, we will see that the first time the user runs the report, it runs really slow and the performance is also bad. It is a good idea to think about some methods to cache the reports so they run faster when the user runs them.

Creating report caching

Mostly all reports are cached by default, but that only happens the first time the user runs the report. Hence, it is better to preload the report so it will be cached and ready when the user wants to run it.

SQL Reporting Services has great caching options that we can take real benefit of.

Before starting to configure the caching options, we need to be sure that Reporting Services has an **Execution Account** connection properly set; this can be validated by running the Reporting Services Configuration manager, going to **Execution Account**, and verifying that there is an account configured as shown in the following screenshot:

We will also need to set the credentials to be stored in the MSCRM_DataSource shared data source by setting the option **Credentials stored securely in the report server** and specifying a username and password.

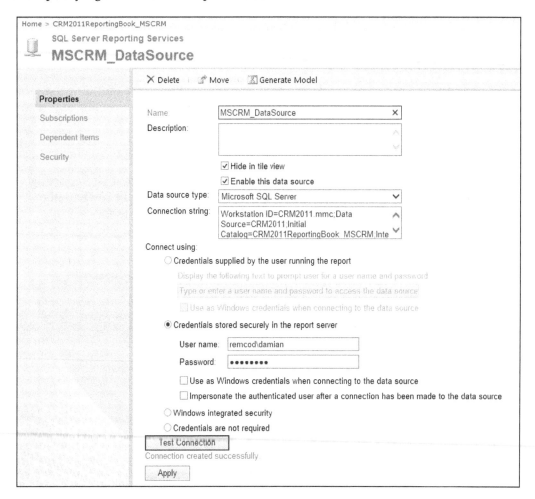

Click on **Test Connection** to make sure that the credentials are okay and then click on **Apply** to save this setting.

Once we have the credentials stored, we can set basic caching options by going to the **Processing Options** tab for the report properties, from where we will be able to set different types of caching. By default, all reports are set to not cache any temporary copy of the report.

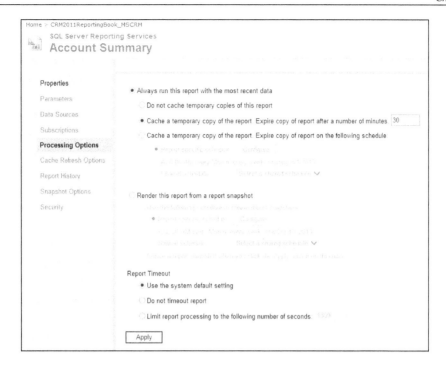

To create better and advanced cache options based on the report parameters, we need to create a cache plan that can be found by going to Report Manager. By going to the properties, we will see the **Cache Refresh Options** tab as shown in the following screenshot:

Click on **New Cache Refresh Plan** to create a new caching rule.

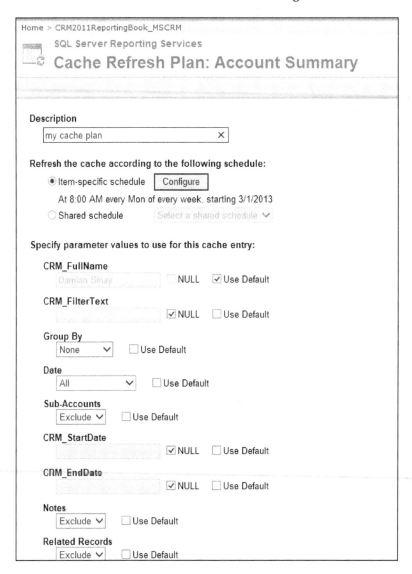

We will be able to use a specific schedule or shared schedule as well as define the options we want cached. The number of options will depend on the number of parameters the report we are configuring has.

Click on **OK** to create the plan. Note that we can have more than one plan defined on the same report with different parameter combinations.

Creating report snapshots

Report snapshots are different from report caching, which are not persisted at the time, in the way they persist. We can have different copies of the report at different times, so we can take a look at these copies and compare them anytime we want because they persist in the database.

In some situations, we can also schedule the reports by creating report snapshots as we saw in the previous chapter. Refer to the *Report Scheduling* recipe of *Chapter 8, Advance Custom Reporting and Automation*. You can also use the **Snapshot Options** tab that is available in the Report Manager application, as shown in the following screenshot:

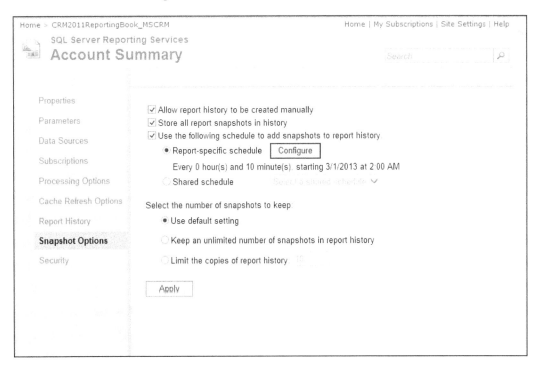

We will be able to use a specific schedule or shared schedule as well as define the options we want the snapshots to be created in.

We then need to click on **Apply** when we are done. We will be able to see the snapshots in the **Report History** option as shown in the following screenshot:

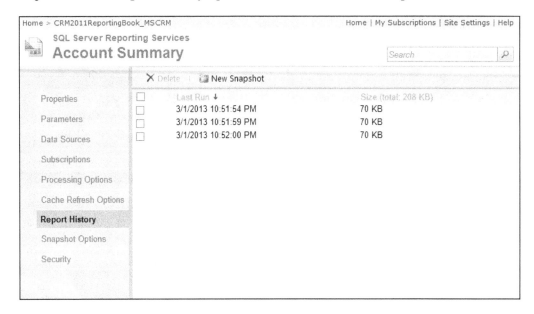

Summary

In this chapter, we looked at how we can troubleshoot different authentication issues we might get when working with reports in Dynamics CRM, and the different ways to improve the performance and deployment of the reports development by using some of the best practices of SQL Reporting Services.

In the next chapter, we are going to see how we can use CRM reports in mobile clients. We are going to see the options we have for the mobile CRM users that want to run and see reports on these types of devices.

10
Mobile Client

In this chapter, we are going to see how we can use the CRM reports in mobile clients. The mobile clients have been growing and are still growing, thanks to the tablet devices. We are going to see the options we have for the mobile CRM users that want to run and see reports on these type of devices.

New features for mobile clients

Since February 2013, when the Update Rollup 12 was released, there were some new features added for the benefit of mobile clients to CRM Online (only) that allow mobile users to use the CRM Online on the iPad, Surface, iPhone, or Windows phone devices. However, the report option is not available for some of these devices and the only reporting options available for now are the dashboards.

Not all the components of the dashboards can be used on these devices; for example, the Silverlight web resources won't work.

 It is also important to know that the versions of the iPad and iPhone need to be iOS 6.0 and above to work. We can use either Safari or Chrome on the iPhone.

There are some commercial client applications for Dynamics CRM (for iPad in the Apple Store); however, I could not find any application that implements the reporting capabilities of CRM 2011. Most of them (such as CWR) can display dashboards such as the CRM Online client on an iPad, but nothing about SSRS reports yet. This is probably going to be a key missing piece that I expect to be covered soon.

Here is an example of how the new mobile client for an iPad looks in CRM Online:

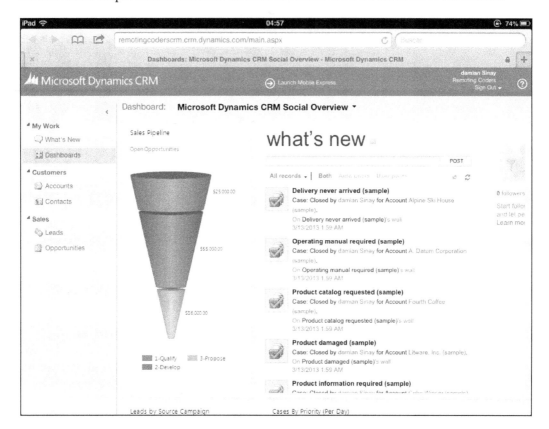

 For more details about the CRM iPad experience, refer to
http://blogs.msdn.com/b/crm/archive/2013/03/01/
crm-for-ipad.aspx.

The site map for this new interface cannot be customized for now, and only the following options will be available:

- **What's New**
- **Dashboards**
- **Accounts**
- **Contacts**
- **Leads**
- **Opportunities**

Clicking on **Launch Mobile Express** will show the same interface the on-premise, with IFD enabled, which the mobile clients will see. The old mobile express interface looks like the following screenshot:

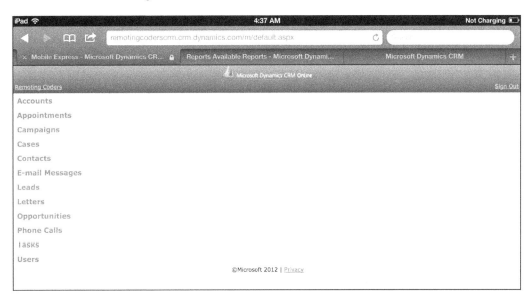

The CRM Online users can now enjoy the new, process-driven UI that will be available on the forms related to the **Contacts**, **Opportunities**, **Leads**, and **Accounts** **(COLA)** entities. The new account form will look as follows on an iPad client device:

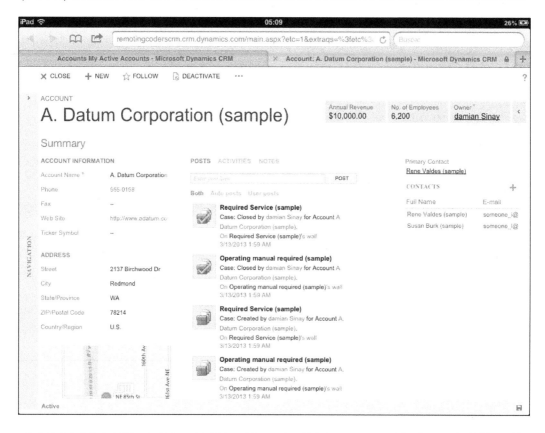

Notice that the forms neither have any ribbon on the top nor any report button. Also, we cannot switch to the classic form if we are on a mobile device such as an iPad.

The sales process

Dynamics CRM 2011 Online now comes with predefined sales processes that help us as a guideline, suggesting the actions we might need to take at each stage of a sale.

The **Opportunities**, **Leads**, and **Cases** entity forms now show a nice section detailing where we are on the sales process. The following screenshot shows this new feature:

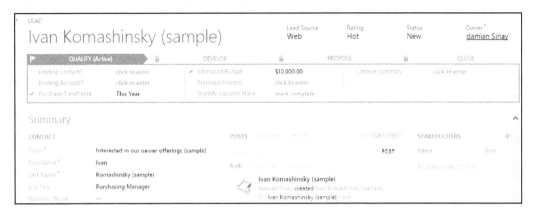

The sales process can be modified by going to a desktop client and clicking on the **Edit Sales Process** link, as shown in the following screenshot:

Clicking on this link will let us define or change the stages of the sales process.

As shown in the following screenshot, the **QUALIFY** stage depends on the **Leads** entity, while all the other predefined stages belong to the **Opportunities** entity:

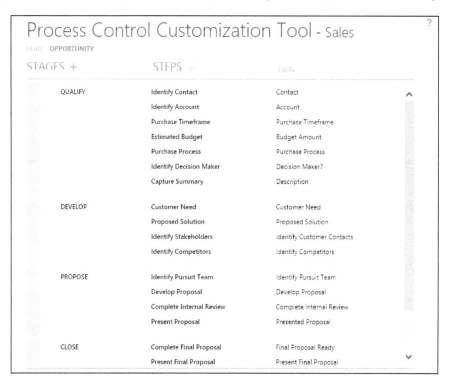

Each stage is comprised of steps and fields from where we can add, remove, or modify to simplify to the end user which field is necessary for each stage of the sales process.

The autosave feature

There is also a new feature added to these new forms called autosave, which automatically saves the form every 30 seconds after a single field change has been made.

Every time a user changes a field, there will be a legend in the bottom of the screen with the text **unsaved changes**:

After 30 seconds, the autosave will fire and the legend will change to **saving**:

Keep in mind that this autosave feature will also fire the following components:

- Plugins
- Workflows
- Record auditing

A more detailed and updated documentation about this new autosave feature can be found in this article: `http://blogs.msdn.com/b/crm/archive/2013/02/18/ auto-save-for-updated-user-experience-forms-in-december-2012-service- update.aspx`.

Even though the report option is not available on the iPad interface, we can add web resources to the new form by customizing it. By going to **Settings | Customizations | Customize the system** from a desktop client, we will see these new forms with the name of the entity we are editing, while the previous or classic ones are called **Information** of type **Main**.

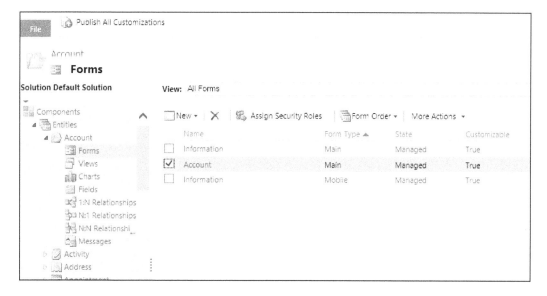

If we install the custom solution we created in *Chapter 6, Creating Inline Reports*, where we created a solution to embed a report on an entity form, we can use that web resource we created to display a report on these new, process-driven UI forms.

A report embedded on the new forms can be seen on an iPad for an account record, as shown in the following screenshot:

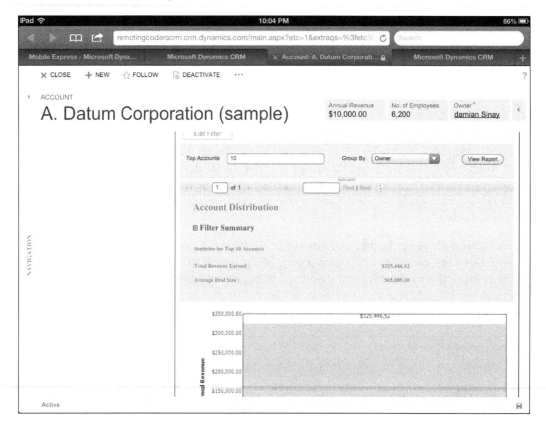

The report can render fine, thanks to the new features of SQL Server 2012 with Service Pack 1, as we will see now in detail.

SQL Server 2012 with SP1

SQL Reporting Services can work on mobile devices if we are using SQL Server 2012 with Service Pack 1. As CRM Online uses this version, we can see the CRM reports by copying the URL of a report and sending it by e-mail.

To do this, open a report in a web browser on a desktop computer first, and copy the URL that you can see in the address bar shown in the following screenshot:

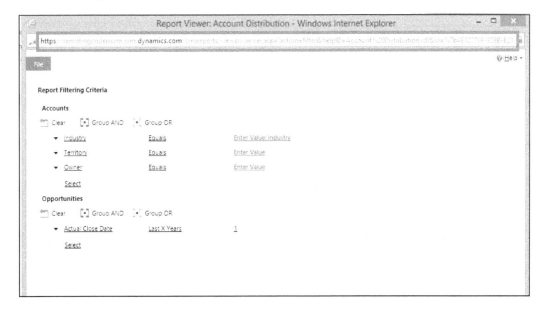

If you don't see the address bar, you can press the *Ctrl + N* keys to open this dialog on a new window that will let us copy the URL address. Then paste this URL address on an e-mail and send it to us or to the user that needs to run the report. The user will then need to read the e-mail from a mobile device, and clicking on the URL will redirect the user to the report interface, from where he will be able to run the report, as shown in the following screenshot:

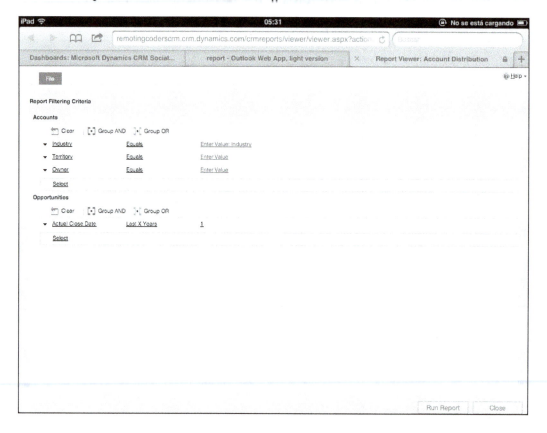

Clicking on **Run Report** will show us the report on the mobile device. Depending on the device, we won't be able to print or export the report to other formats such as XML, CSV, PDF, MHTML, Excel, TIFF, and Word.

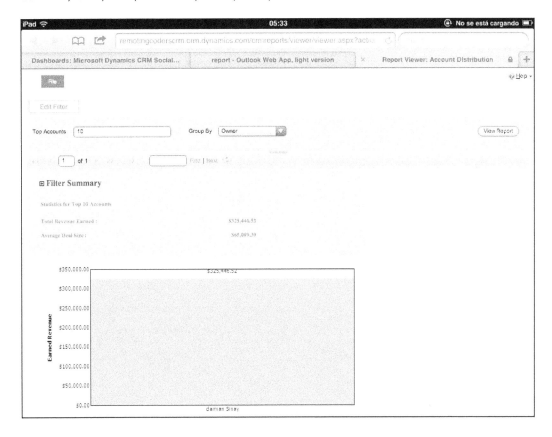

Microsoft Surface

On the other hand, if we use a device such as Microsoft Surface, the report's options are available on the site map and we will be able to use them directly from the main web interface.

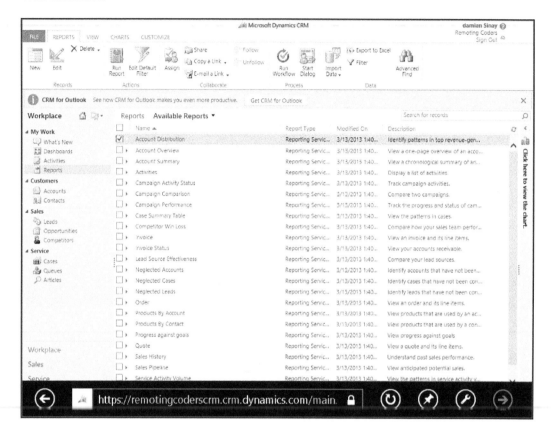

As we can see, the Dynamics CRM web interface runs pretty well on a Microsoft Surface device, not showing the same limitations as we saw in the iPad; this is basically because the Surface device uses Internet Explorer 10.

The mobile client's considerations

The client interfaces that we have seen earlier require the user to be connected to the Internet, and they don't work in an offline mode.

There are some considerations to keep in mind if our environment uses CRM on premise, and we want to let our user access the CRM data externally using the mobile devices.

Authentication considerations

Most of the mobile clients will be located outside the local network; so if we are working with an on-premise environment, we will have to enable **Internet-Facing Deployment** (**IFD**). This means we need to change the authentication method from an integrated windows authentication to a claims-based authentication that requires the deployment of the **Active Directory Federation Service** (**ADFS**).

Enabling a claims-based authentication will also force us to implement the HTTPS protocol that will also require us to purchase an SSL certificate. A 2048-bits SSL certificate is recommended. It can be obtained on `Verigin.com` or `Godaddy.com`, among other SSL certificate providers.

Depending on the number of organizations we have, we will need to get a certificate that allows different **Subject Alternative Names** (**SAN**), or better a wildcard certificate, so that the number of organizations is not limited.

So, we need to store this SSL certificate on the Dynamics CRM server and on the ADFS server if we have them in separate boxes. First, configure the certificate on the IIS on both servers, and then for CRM, use the Microsoft Dynamics CRM Deployment Manager application. Click on the **Microsoft Dynamics CRM** root node on the left-hand side and on **Properties** on the right-hand side. Then, change to **Web Addresses** to configure the **HTTPS** protocol, as shown in the following screenshot:

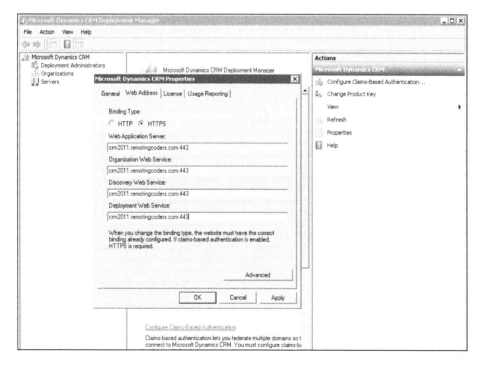

Once we configure the HTTPS, we will be allowed to click on the **Configure Claims-Based Authentication** link on the right-hand panel. This will start a wizard that will require us to enter the federation URL of the ADFS server, which would be similar to `https://sts.remotingcoders.com/FederationMetadata/2007-06/federationmetadata.xml`.

After we close this wizard, we will need to click on another link that appears on the right-hand panel named **Configure Internet-Facing Deployment...**, which will open another wizard where we will need to configure the web application server's domain, the organization server's domain, and the discovery web service's domain.

This is all we need to do on the CRM box; then there are some configurations we will need to make on the ADFS server, which require the creation of Relaying Party Trust, where we will need to pass a URL provided by Dynamics CRM's claims-based authentication at the end of the first wizard. It should be similar to `https://crm.remotingcoders.com/FederationMetadata/2007-06/federationmetadata.xml`.

By enabling these types of authentications, external users will be able to log in to the CRM with a secure, forms-based authentication page:

Configuring IFD on Dynamics CRM 2011 is a very complex task; however, we can find a lot of videos on YouTube that show how to configure this properly — just do a search of CRM 2011 IFD. For additional technical information, we can check `http://technet.microsoft.com/en-us/library/gg188579.aspx`.

Custom reports development considerations

When we develop custom reports that are to be used by mobile clients, it is recommended to use HTML 5 and a cross browser JavaScript framework such as jQuery. We need to stay away from using Silverlight or ActiveX controls, as they are not supported on mobile devices.

All the latest tablets and smartphones such as the iPad, Surface, and Android support HTML5, CSS3, and JavaScript, so using these languages is the best option.

With the new capabilities of SSRS with SQL Server 2012 R2, we can now embed the SSRS report control on custom ASP.NET applications that will render the reports in the HTML5 mode.

Some functionalities such as exporting or printing the report will be missing on iPads, so that is something we will have to custom-develop if we have that requirement at present.

Summary

In this chapter, we looked at the new features of Dynamics CRM and SQL Server SP1 to show and run reports on mobile devices such as the iPhone, iPad, and Surface. We looked at how to configure the IFD authentication, so we can give external users access to our on-premise CRM environment.

In the following appendix, we are going to see basic and advanced reporting services' expressions; we can use them to show data in different ways and formats. We are also going to see some user interactions with reports for handling some of the common mouse click events.

Expression Snippets

In this appendix, we are going to see the basic and advanced Reporting Services expressions that we can use to show data in different ways and formats. We are also going to look at some user interactions with the reports to handle some of the common mouse click events.

Basic expressions

With expressions, we are talking about the Microsoft SQL Server Reporting Server expressions that we can use from either the Visual Studio Report editor or with the SQL Report Builder tool.

The basic expressions are grouped in the following categories:

- Constants
- Built-in fields
- Parameters
- Fields
- Datasets
- Variables
- Operators
  - Arithmetic (^, *, /, \, Mod, +, -)
  - Comparison (<, <=, >, >=, =, <>, Like, Is)
  - Concatenation (&, +)
  - Logical bitwise (And, Not, Or, AndAlso, OrElse)
  - Bit Shift (<<, >>)

- Common Functions

  - Text
  - Date and Time
  - Math
  - Inspection
  - Program Flow
  - Aggregate
  - Financial
  - Conversion
  - Miscellaneous

The basic expressions are available in the **Expression** editor dialog box, as shown in the following screenshot:

Constants

The **Constants** option will show you all the constants you have defined for your report. Constants are useful if you want to avoid using values in your expressions that would not make sense in a big piece of code. For example, asking if a variable such as status equals zero is not the same as saying the variable status equals active. In that case, creating a constant for the active value would be defined as follows:

```
Public Const Active As Int32 = 0
```

You can define constants in the **Code** section. You can access the **Code** section by going to the **Report | Report Properties** menu in Visual Studio.

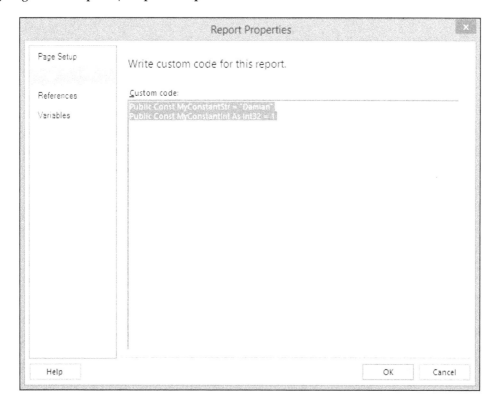

A custom code for this report is as follows:

```
Public Const MyConstantStr = "Damian"
Public Const MyConstantInt As Int32 = 1
```

Notice that these constants might not be displayed in the **Constants** category, but you can still use them in the **Expression** editor as follows:

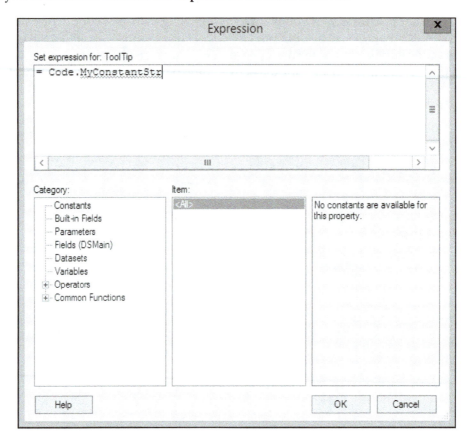

For example, the expression set for ToolTip is as follows:

```
= Code.MyConstantStr
```

Variables

You can define global variables in the **Variables** section, which you can access by going to the **Report** | **Report Properties** menu in Visual Studio. Variables can be read only; in that case, they will be similar to constants and they can also contain expressions.

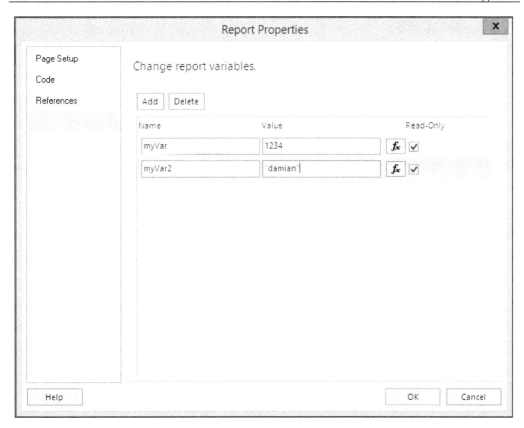

You can then use the variables as follows:

```
= Variables!myVar.Value
```

Advanced expressions with VBScript code

Most of the time, you will be able to meet your report requirements using the basic and out of the box functions in your expressions editor; if you need to make more complex functions, you can write your own or use references as we will see next.

References

You can also add references to the .NET assemblies. Depending on the version of SQL Server you are using, you will be able to add assemblies. For example, you can add the assemblies created for the .NET framework 3.5 if you are working with SQL 2008 or for the .NET framework 4.0 in SQL 2012.

You can add references in the **References** section by going to the **Report | Report Properties** menu in Visual Studio. There you will be able to select an assembly that is installed on the **GAC (Global Assembly Cache)** or browse it from your local drives.

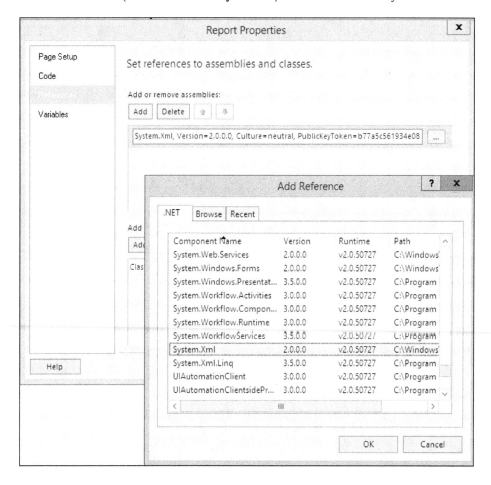

For example, you can add the `System.Xml` assembly if you need to manage the XML code in your report. Then you can use it in the expressions by writing a function in the **Code** section of the **Report Properties** window, as shown in the following code:

```
Public Function GetName()
  Dim mydoc as new  System.Xml.XmlDocument
  mydoc.LoadXml("<root><customer>damain</customer></root>")
  Dim node as System.Xml.XmlNode
  node = mydoc.SelectSingleNode("/root/customer")
  Return node.InnerText
End Function
```

Then you can use this function on any expression as follows:

```
= Code.GetName()
```

You can also add references to the custom assemblies, which you create with Visual Studio; in that case you need to be sure that your assembly is signed by a strong key and you copy that assembly on the SSRS server by either installing it on the GAC or in the Report Server's `bin` folder, which is usually located at `C:\Program Files\ Microsoft SQL Server\MSSQL\Reporting Services\ReportServer\bin`. You will also need to edit `web.config` to add a reference to your custom assembly as follows:

```
<CodeGroup
  class="FirstMatchCodeGroup"
  version="1"
  PermissionSetName="FullTrust"
  Name="MyCustomAssemblyCodeGroup"
Description="A special code group for my custom assembly.">
  <IMembershipCondition
    class="UrlMembershipCondition"
    version="1"
  Url="C:\Program Files\Microsoft SQL Server\MSSQL\Reporting
  Services\ReportServer\bin\CustomAssembly.dll"/>
</CodeGroup>
```

Working with control events

Controls in Reporting Services have some limited interactivity with the users; this is because they are mostly intended to be used to show and report data with no interactivity as you would have on a custom application, where the user can interact with controls such as buttons, checkboxes, or radio buttons. That is why you will see these types of controls missing in the report items' toolbox.

Actions

You can add some interactivity by using the **Actions** section of Placeholder Properties as follows:

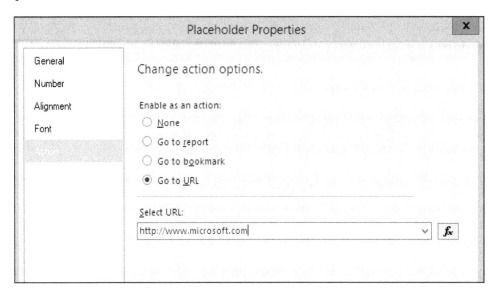

The options of **Action** are:

- **None**
- **Go to report**
- **Go to bookmark**
- **Go to URL**

Using this will be similar to handling the click event of any report control. To add a bookmark on your report, just place a **Textbox** control and go to the **Properties** window; there you will find the **bookmark** property, where you will be able to add a name.

Visibility

Another way to handle the click event is by using the **Visibility** section and checking the **Display can be toggled by this report item:** option. This option will also handle the user's mouse click event to show or hide other controls on your report.

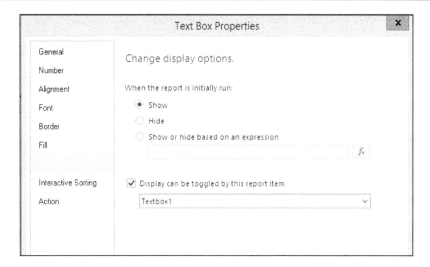

Interactive Sorting

Interactive Sorting adds another way to let the user interact with the report by allowing sorting of columns on a table. This way the user can change the default sorting presented by clicking on the column header of the table. Clicking on the header once will sort the records in ascending order, while clicking on it a second time will sort the reports in descending order.

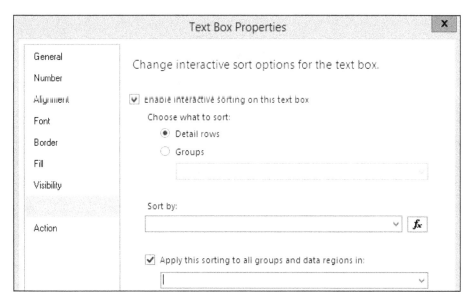

After enabling sorting, a table would look as follows:

accountnumber		accountid	name	createdon
BTBS3G34		22fdd1a6-3aa0-e211-9403-00155dfe080f	Unusual Store (sample)	4/8/2013 7:54:23 AM
BO8C3J9U		1efdd1a6-3aa0-e211-9403-00155dfe080f	Magnificent Store (sample)	4/8/2013 7:54:23 AM

Summary

In this appendix, we looked at the basic expressions, and how we can use them in our reports; we learned how to use constants, variables, and functions as well as using external .NET assemblies by using references. Finally we looked at the user interaction controls that give us some interaction with the users.

Index

F

G

H

I

J

L

M

Thank you for buying
Microsoft Dynamics CRM 2011 Reporting

About Packt Publishing

Packt, pronounced 'packed', published its first book "Mastering phpMyAdmin for Effective MySQL Management" in April 2004 and subsequently continued to specialize in publishing highly focused books on specific technologies and solutions.

Our books and publications share the experiences of your fellow IT professionals in adapting and customizing today's systems, applications, and frameworks. Our solution based books give you the knowledge and power to customize the software and technologies you're using to get the job done. Packt books are more specific and less general than the IT books you have seen in the past. Our unique business model allows us to bring you more focused information, giving you more of what you need to know, and less of what you don't.

Packt is a modern, yet unique publishing company, which focuses on producing quality, cutting-edge books for communities of developers, administrators, and newbies alike. For more information, please visit our website: www.packtpub.com.

About Packt Enterprise

In 2010, Packt launched two new brands, Packt Enterprise and Packt Open Source, in order to continue its focus on specialization. This book is part of the Packt Enterprise brand, home to books published on enterprise software – software created by major vendors, including (but not limited to) IBM, Microsoft and Oracle, often for use in other corporations. Its titles will offer information relevant to a range of users of this software, including administrators, developers, architects, and end users.

Writing for Packt

We welcome all inquiries from people who are interested in authoring. Book proposals should be sent to author@packtpub.com. If your book idea is still at an early stage and you would like to discuss it first before writing a formal book proposal, contact us; one of our commissioning editors will get in touch with you.

We're not just looking for published authors; if you have strong technical skills but no writing experience, our experienced editors can help you develop a writing career, or simply get some additional reward for your expertise.

Microsoft Dynamics CRM 2011
New Features

ISBN: 978-1-849682-06-0   Paperback: 288 pages

Get up to spend with the new features of Microsoft
Dynamics CRM 2011

1. Master the new features of Microsoft
   Dynamics 2011

2. Use client-side programming to perform
   data validation, automation, and process
   enhancement

3. Learn powerful event driven server-side
   programming methods: Plug-Ins and
   Processes (Formerly Workflows)

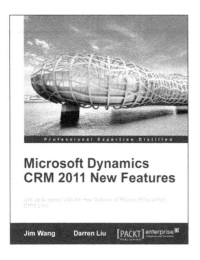

Microsoft Dynamics CRM 2011
Application Design

ISBN: 978-1-849684-56-9   Paperback: 236 pages

Develop applictaions for any situation with our
hands-on guide to Microsoft Dynamics CRM 2011

1. Create your first application quickly and with
   no fuss

2. Develop in days what it has taken others years

3. Provide the solution to your company's
   problems

Please check **www.PacktPub.com** for information on our titles

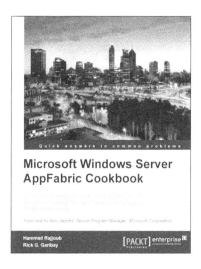

Microsoft Windows Server
AppFabric Cookbook

Microsoft Windows Server AppFabric Cookbook

ISBN: 978-1-849684-18-7   Paperback: 428 pages

60 recipes for getting the most out of WCF and WF services, including the latest capabilities in AppFabric 1.1 for Windows Server

1. Gain a solid understanding of the capabilities provided by Windows Server AppFabric with a pragmatic, hands-on, results-oriented approach with this book and eBook

2. Learn how to apply the WCF and WF skills you already have to make the most of what Windows Server AppFabric has to offer

3. Includes step-by-step recipes for developing highly scalable composite services that utilize the capabilities provided by Windows Server AppFabric including caching, hosting, monitoring and persistence

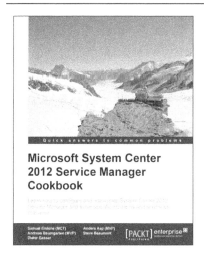

Microsoft System Center
2012 Service Manager
Cookbook

Microsoft System Center 2012 Service Manager Cookbook

ISBN: 978-1-849686-94-5   Paperback: 474 pages

Learn how to configure and administer System Center 2012 Service Manager and solve specific problems and scenarios that arise

1. Practical cookbook with recipes that will help you get the most out of Microsoft System Center 2012 Service Manager

2. Learn the various methods and best practices administrating and using Microsoft System Center 2012 Service Manager

Please check **www.PacktPub.com** for information on our titles